ADVERTISING AGENCY AND STUDIO SKILLS

THIRD EDITION
REVISED AND UPDATED
ILLUSTRATED BY THE AUTHOR

ADVERTISING AGENCY AND STUDIO SKILLS
by Tom Cardamone

WATSON-GUPTILL PUBLICATIONS / NEW YORK

To Debra

Copyright © 1981 by Watson-Guptill Publications

First published 1981 by Watson-Guptill Publications,
a division of Billboard Publications, Inc.,
1515 Broadway, New York, N.Y. 10036

Library of Congress Cataloging in Publication Data

Cardamone, Tom.
   Advertising agency and studio skills.
Includes index.
   1. Advertising layout and typography.
2. Commercial art.   I. Title.
HF5825.C29   1981   659.13′24   80-27166
ISBN 0-8230-0151-2

Manufactured in U.S.A.

First Edition
   First Printing, 1959
   Second Printing, 1961
   Third Printing, 1964
   Fourth Printing, 1967
   Fifth Printing, 1968
Second Edition, Revised and Enlarged
   First Printing, 1970
   Second Printing, 1973
   Third Printing, 1975
   Fourth Printing, 1976
   Fifth Printing, 1977
   Sixth Printing, 1978
Third Edition, Revised and Updated
   First Printing, 1981

FOREWORD

Board procedure for artists in agencies and studios encompasses numerous skills and techniques. One category of this procedure is referred to as "mechanicals," which, although it is essentially a subject within itself, is yet so interrelated with all other aspects of board procedure that it is difficult to define. Because the subject requires so vast a knowledge of advertising, it is fast becoming a necessary prerequisite to gaining a foothold in the broad field of advertising. Keen competition makes it difficult for the average student, at the onset of his or her career, to obtain a first position in the capacity desired. There is little time to break in the beginner—who must already have some knowledge of the business, not just creative ability. In order to produce the desired effect, which is the result of advertising "know-how," the beginner must first accumulate certain specific information and experience.

While the student (as well as the already developed artist) is making every effort to find a position that will present an opportunity for self-expression, he or she must reach out in every direction for additional, more extensive knowledge and understanding, in order to nurture latent creativity, as well as manual capabilities.

Quite often, people who do mechanicals are not considered creative artists. They are sometimes looked upon as ordinary machine operators in a factory. This attitude, of course, is fallacious. An employer may say, "Mechanical artists? They're expendable." An experienced artist may say, "Mechanicals? There's nothing to it! You can learn it in two weeks." These people have either forgotten how long it takes to learn all the requirements of this position, or are kidding themselves into thinking they know all that it involves. For if they deliberated the requirements of the artist who produces mechanicals, they would realize that to achieve the true expertness of an all-round professional takes a good deal of experience and hard work. Artists must not only develop manual dexterity, they must possess unlimited knowledge of advertising procedure. They are technicians as well as artists, and their product, the mechanical, affords the employer a fair profit.

The increasing demand for good mechanical (or board) artists is becoming more apparent every day within our studios and agencies, owing to the growing realization of their importance. (For the sake of clarifying the distinction between the "mechanical" and the "board" artist, you might consider the board artist as being the more advanced, all-round professional of the two.) It is my purpose in writing this book not only to offer valuable information for the artist, but also to acquaint the upper echelon with the qualifications of the mechanical and board professional.

By and large, it is not necessary to possess any special artistic talent in order to learn mechanicals. Essentially, it is a manual technique used in conjunction with certain information. Naturally, the more knowledge and experience at his or her command, the more efficient the mechanical artist will be. But there is one thing that separates the ordinary from the professional and that is *judgment* in the preparation of mechanicals. The artist's esthetic sense plays an important role in the development of good judgment. This is something that cannot be taught in a book—it must be developed through experience.

While the artist has much to offer mechanicals, it is fortunate that mechanicals offer more, in return, to the artist. During the process of learning this procedure, the artist is developing skill in handling tools and equipment, and increasing knowledge of advertising makeup; he or she is exposed to new areas of the advertising business. A thorough knowledge of mechanicals has enabled many artists to gain entrance into a variety of jobs in the advertising field. The extensive discipline mechanicals provide allows artists trained in this area to choose from many different—and attractive—possibilities. Some artists may not want to be illustrators after all, or an art director's position may no longer be appealing—some may have acquired an appetite for production or studio managing. Perhaps some would rather sell art than prepare it, and others might even start their own studios.

With the advance of methods and means, the business of advertising has become a many-faceted composite of esthetic, educated, progressive, and hard-working men and women. Its energy is expended the world over. The artist as a creator of mechanicals is an essential gear within this machinery, without whom production could not continue at its present volume.

This book represents an accumulation of information that would take considerable time at school and experience in the field to obtain. It is a foundation for the beginner and a source of further information for the already experienced artist, upon which can be built a pleasant and fruitful future in advertising.

However, the content of this book alone is not the answer to your future as an artist; rather, regard it as a vehicle for advancement toward creative expression. The development of these technical skills will enhance your opportunities for making a living, but this use of tools, materials, and accumulation of technical knowledge should serve only as a medium for the construction of cultural contributions.

It isn't enough to be a competent technician in the art field, whether it be commercial or otherwise. Artists carry the responsibility of contributing to contemporary society. They must create and cultivate new meanings and formulas. They must broaden their scope of ethics and philosophy so that their graphic communication with the world may function as a nourishing influence toward its cultural development. Do not be content with having acquired manual dexterity or technical proficiency, but enthusiastically launch yourself into further studies in the related fields of graphic expression.

CONTENTS

INTRODUCTION

In order that you may visualize the mechanical artist's part in advertising makeup, I have briefly summarized the general steps taken to produce an advertisement in agencies and studios. They are as follows:

The client has a product to advertise.

The client contacts the account executive at a particular advertising agency.

The account executive, in turn, confers with the copywriter, art director, or creative director.

The account executive proposes a plan to the client, which, after due consideration and approval, is put into effect.

Copy is written for the client's approval.

The art director prepares layouts or roughs for client approval. In many cases, a more comprehensive layout is prepared.

After an o.k. from the client, the type is ordered, and usually the art director and account executive discuss (with the production manager) proper procedure for execution, according to budget and time.

The production manager confers with the platemakers and printers to estimate costs.

The artist is given the layout, together with its mechanical instructions and components.

After the mechanical has been prepared, it may be sent back to the client for further consideration. If no changes are necessary, the mechanical is then sent to the platemaker.

After plates are made, three or four proofs are sent to the production manager for final checkup and possible change before printing the required quantity.

If the proofs meet with the approval of the production manager and everyone concerned, the printer completes the run.

Now that you know your position as a mechanical artist, you can readily understand your importance and responsibility. To begin with, the advertisement cannot be produced without some sort of "mechanical art assembly" that corresponds with the layout. What appears in the mechanical will appear in final printing. Should there be an error (on anyone's part) in this mechanical, it could be quite costly. Therefore, it is the obligation of the mechanical artist to see to it that all the requirements of the job are fulfilled with complete accuracy and understanding.

The work procedure described throughout this book is directed toward studio and agency operation dealing in high-level work—*quality*, not *economy*. It is my contention that artists who have been taught the execution of superior work will have no difficulty learning the cheaper, sometimes quicker, and less skillful approach. But artists who start their careers in this lower echelon will go through a good deal of struggling to attain the upper level of quality.

CHAPTER 1

PASTE-UPS

Paste-up artists are usually apprentices. Their duties deal mostly with the preparation of dummies, mounting photos and art, cutting mats (frames) for art, pasting up assemblies for various presentations, etc. Generally, they have nothing to do with mechanicals.

A *paste-up mechanical* (or simply a mechanical) is art prepared in paste-up form, specifically for reproduction in strict accordance with a layout or dummy under the supervision of an art director.

LAYOUTS, DUMMIES, ART

An idea is conceived for an advertisement with specific conditions, and small, rough sketches, called *thumbnails*, are worked out in searching for an appropriate layout. Using the thumbnail as a guide, the art director will draw an actual-size "layout" of his idea. The layout may be either roughly indicated or "worked up" enough to present a fairly concise visual idea of the arrangement. A mechanical is made, using this layout as a guide.

Very often the client will want to see a more thorough visualization of the idea or layout. In such cases, with the layout as a guide, a comprehensive ("comp") is made. The comp looks as close to the finished printed job as possible. With this comp as a guide, the mechanical is made.

For folders, mailing pieces, brochures, etc., the actual piece is constructed by hand, according to the layout in comprehensive form, and presented to the client. This is called a "dummy," and it is also followed in the preparation of the mechanical.

"Art" does not necessarily mean a drawing or painting. Any finished piece that is to be used for reproduction is considered art. Many also refer to art as "copy."

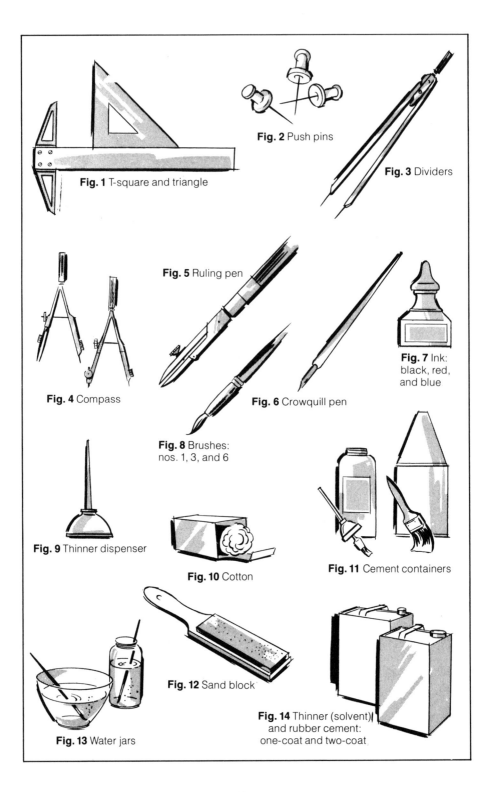

Fig. 1 T-square and triangle

Fig. 2 Push pins

Fig. 3 Dividers

Fig. 5 Ruling pen

Fig. 4 Compass

Fig. 6 Crowquill pen

Fig. 7 Ink: black, red, and blue

Fig. 8 Brushes: nos. 1, 3, and 6

Fig. 9 Thinner dispenser

Fig. 10 Cotton

Fig. 11 Cement containers

Fig. 12 Sand block

Fig. 13 Water jars

Fig. 14 Thinner (solvent) and rubber cement: one-coat and two-coat

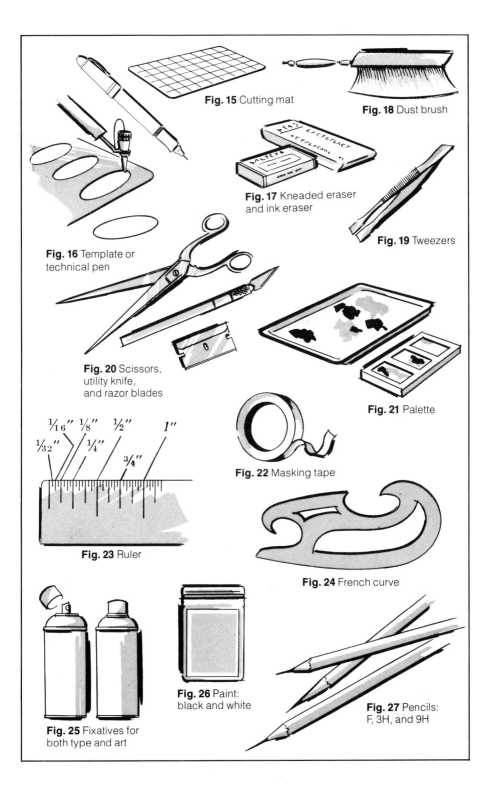

Fig. 15 Cutting mat

Fig. 18 Dust brush

Fig. 16 Template or technical pen

Fig. 17 Kneaded eraser and ink eraser

Fig. 19 Tweezers

Fig. 20 Scissors, utility knife, and razor blades

Fig. 21 Palette

$\frac{1}{32}''$ $\frac{1}{16}''$ $\frac{1}{8}''$ $\frac{1}{4}''$ $\frac{1}{2}''$ $\frac{3}{4}''$ $1''$

Fig. 22 Masking tape

Fig. 23 Ruler

Fig. 24 French curve

Fig. 26 Paint: black and white

Fig. 25 Fixatives for both type and art

Fig. 27 Pencils: F, 3H, and 9H

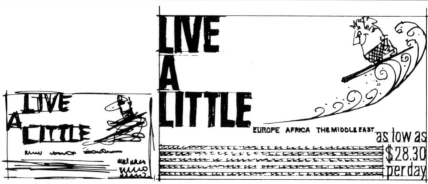

Fig. 28 Thumbnail.　　**Fig. 29** Layout

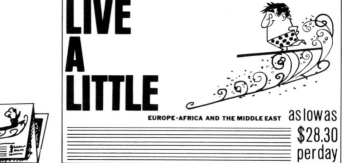

Fig. 30 The art work is made actual size in the dummy.　**Fig. 31** The comp looks like the piece reproduced.

MATERIALS AND TOOLS

Because of the variety of work and problems encountered each day in advertising, there is actually no limit to the number and types of tools and equipment used. However, there are certain materials needed for the average, everyday job, without which the artist's capabilities are limited. Illustrated on the preceding pages are such tools. Learn to know how and when to use them properly.

PAPER STOCK

Listed here are the papers and boards you will work with almost every day. There are others, but these are the most widely used:

Bond paper (ledger bond): a smooth, opaque, white paper. It comes in three weights: light, medium, and heavy. Bond may be used for line drawings, masks, flaps, dummies, and comprehensives.

Visual layout bond: a "toothy," translucent white paper used in preparing comps, layouts, and dummies. Excellent for sketching with color markers.

Tracing paper: an almost transparent paper having unlimited uses, but mainly for layouts, color indications on art or mechanicals, flaps, slip-sheets, etc.

Illustration board: available in a variety of makes, grades, and surfaces. Generally two types of surfaces will serve you: rough and smooth. Rough surfaced boards are used in mechanicals that do not require clean line inking, all types of finished art work, and comps. The smooth surfaced boards are used for mechanicals demanding smooth, clean line work, for many styles of finished art, for mounting photos or art, and for comps.

Strathmore: a high-grade drawing paper available in various weights. It is primarily used for art work, but it can also be used for mechanicals and dummies. Excellent for inking.

Matboard (pebble board): also made in a variety of surfaces. However, it has its peculiarities. It is a soft, inferior grade of board and should be used with discretion. Do not mount a photo on pebble board, as it might leave a textured impression on the photo that may interfere with reproduction. Its main use is for matting (framing) art and layouts. It may be used for art work when a particular technique is sought. *Never* use pebble board for a mechanical.

Mounting board: usually smooth and of substantial weight. Used for mounting or backing up photos or art.

Color background paper: available in many brands, this is simply a sheet of paper colored on one side. Because it comes in a very wide range of hues and tints, it has untold uses.

Color film sheet: a clear, lightweight, colored acetate which is coated on the back with a waxlike adhesive. Available in many colors and tints, it is especially useful for preparing layouts and dummies. (One good use, for example, is the creation of smooth color backgrounds or panels.) It is also used for color separation on mechanicals. Because it is transparent, it presents an excellent visualization of the effects desired.

Screen or texture sheets (available in many brands): thin, clear acetate film having a "line" (black or white) texture or pattern printed on one side. Formerly known as Ben Day sheets, these have an adhesive backing. The sheet is placed onto a mechanical or art, and the desired shape is cut out and burnished. This is especially useful where "tone" effects are desired on "line" art. (See Chapter 4.)

Vellum: a heavy tracing paper used for tracing, art work, and in the preparation of overlays for color separation on mechanicals and art. Ink or paint can be scratched off with a razor blade for corrections and special effects.

Acetate: frosted or clear, available in different weights, used for color separation overlays and art. Ink can be scratched off for special effects or corrections.

Masking film (or litho film): a clear polyester backing sheet coated on one side with a thin stripping film. Usually available in one or two colors— ruby or amber—this film is used primarily for color separation. The color film, which constitutes the mask, is cut and peeled away from the clear polyester, exposing the areas to be printed.

LIGHT TABLE

Some artists just cannot get along without a light table. While it is not an absolute necessity, it offers innumerable advantages. If you feel the cost of a commercial light table is beyond your present capacity, it is simple to make your own. You might try converting an old drawing table into one. This is very convenient. When not in use as a light table, place a board over it and use it as a drawing table (Fig. 32).

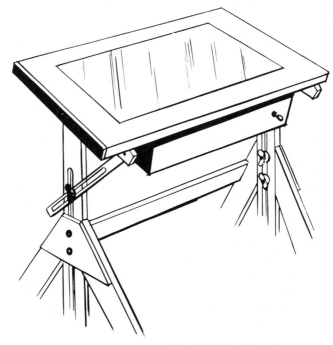

Fig. 32 Light table.

RAZOR BLADES

Razor blades do not retain their sharpness very long. As a matter of fact, one lasts long enough to cut only one mat. Always use a fresh blade when cutting something important. *Caution:* it is dangerous to manipulate elements during a paste-up (such as type) with the corner of the blade edge. The tip of the blade may snap off and fly in your face. If you must use a razor for this, try the corner of the back edge (single-edged razor blade), but be careful or you may cut your finger.

POLAROID CAMERA

A Polaroid camera is unquestionably useful in figure work as well as in drawing objects or products. It is also used in the preparation of layouts or comps. You can photostat the Polaroid print to suit your needs. This can be a tremendous time saver.

PASTE-UP METHODS

To execute a proper paste-up, the consistency of the rubber cement is very important. If you use two-coat cement, a mixture of four parts cement to one part benzine or thinner will give proper results. The cement should be thin enough to flow freely from the brush.

There are several methods of pasting up. One way is to apply the rubber cement to the surfaces of both pieces and allow this to dry, then adhere. Another method is to apply the cement to one surface; let it dry; cement the other surface; and, while it is still wet, paste together. The beginner should follow this last method. Yet another method is to apply the cement to one side only and paste up while still wet. This is a quick but not very permanent paste-up and should be used with discretion.

Excess rubber cement can be rubbed off with your finger or with an eraser, but the most practical method is with the "pickup." This is simply a ball of rubber cement accumulated from around the edges of the cement container. A ready-made pickup is also available.

SLIPSHEET METHOD—TWO-COAT CEMENT

Owing to the extreme tackiness of rubber cement, it is sometimes difficult to paste large or flimsy material without its buckling or wrinkling. Therefore, the "slipsheet" method is used.

First, cement both surfaces and allow to dry. Then, cover the area to be mounted upon with a clean piece of tissue paper, leaving about ½" of exposed cement at the top or narrowest end (Fig. 33). Dry cement will not adhere to a noncemented surface. Holding the piece to be mounted at both ends, place it upon the tissue, permitting it to adhere lightly to the ½" exposed area (Fig. 34).

Being certain that the mounted sheet is flat and tacked into proper position, slide the tissue from beneath, gradually smoothing it with your

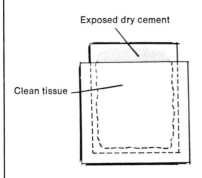

Exposed dry cement

Clean tissue

Fig. 33 When you rubber cement with the slipsheet method, the tissue must cover all of the remaining cemented area.

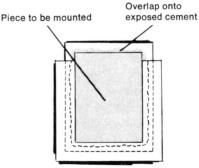

Piece to be mounted

Overlap onto exposed cement

Fig. 34 Press the piece firmly at the top when you slide the tissue from below.

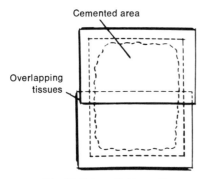

Cemented area

Overlapping tissues

Fig. 35 Only a slight overlap.

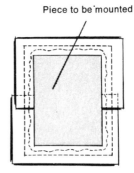

Piece to be mounted

Fig. 36 Pull out the bottom tissue first.

hand outward from the center. Then cover with a clean sheet of paper and burnish air pockets and creases outward from the center. For burnishing, you can use a flat straightedge, such as a plastic triangle. However, burnishing with a plastic device tends to melt or burn away its edge as a result of heat created by the friction, thus destroying the efficiency of the tool. Therefore, keep on hand a triangle to be used only for this purpose.

For mounting large sheets, two tissues are used, overlapping about ½" at the center. The same procedure is employed, slipping out first one tissue, then the other (Figs. 35 and 36).

REMOVING A MOUNTED SHEET
In order to remove a mounted sheet, use thinner (applied with a thinner dispenser), carefully lifting the surface to be removed while pouring. It is

very important that the cemented surfaces be clean and free of dirt particles, or impressions will appear after remounting. Sometimes thinner will stain a surface; however, in most instances the stain will be temporary and will dry out in a short time.

ONE-COAT CEMENT

Since *one-coat* cement has become such a part of the artist's materials, the cement referred to above is now commonly called *two-coat* or *regular* rubber cement. One-coat is a much tackier rubber cement which requires only one application to the back of the unit to be mounted.

Many artists consider one-coat a faster and cleaner way to work, because of the relative freedom of manipulation of the unit and the elimination of excess cement clean-up. After the cement has dried, the art is properly positioned, then simply burnished into place.

If the unit has to be repositioned or lifted, use the corner of a razor blade to pull away one corner of the art and lift it with your tweezers. If the art has been burnished too firmly, apply thinner along the edges to loosen it before lifting. Then reposition and burnish. There is no need to recement the unit. But be careful to avoid tearing the art.

You will find one-coat extremely useful for replacing small units or for correcting misspelled words or punctuation. Using it for pasting up on acetate lessens the chore considerably. You'll also find it most helpful in pasting up dummies and layouts.

There are, however, certain aspects of using one-coat that may be troublesome. Because of its extreme tackiness, you'll find it difficult to slipsheet large units; it sticks to the slipsheet. Try using the wax paper found in the back of some tracing pads or bond pads.

If you turn over a unit with dried one-coat cement on the back, you'll find it will stick to the surface. This is troublesome and may occur frequently when you want to cut the art. Using waxed paper between the unit and the board you're cutting on does not really help. Use a piece of clean vinyl as a cutting board, or make your own: remove the back cardboard from a pad and completely cover one side with masking tape, overlapping each strip slightly.

A worthwhile investment would be to purchase a cutting mat which is made specifically for one-coat cement. It should last for several months under heavy use (Fig. 15).

One last thing about one-coat cement as a word of caution. Its unusually adhesive qualities can create a mess in your files or on your work table because it sticks to anything it touches. Excess pieces thrown haphazardly around your work area can stick to something important and you may throw it away. Razor blades can get caught up in the sticky waste on your table, and you may unwittingly cut yourself when crumpling pieces of paper to be thrown away.

There will be occasions when you'll have to remove cement from the back of a unit for one reason or another. This could be quite a problem inasmuch as the pickup will stick to the cement, making it difficult to pull away without tearing the unit. Try this: coat the unit with *two-coat* cement (directly over the one-coat) and let it dry. Then proceed to remove the cement with your pickup in the regular manner.

SPRAY CAN ADHESIVE

The cement in spray cans is similar to one-coat and is used in the same manner. Although exceptionally useful when mounting very large units, the excess spray does drift into the surrounding areas of the unit being sprayed. This can be quite messy and, needless to say, destructive. Use it with care, being certain to have a sheet of newspaper or something comparable behind the unit to protect the surrounding areas.

If not used frequently, and if not maintained, the spray button on these cans clogs with cement and often breaks down.

DOUBLE-COATED ADHESIVE FILM

Double-coated, pressure-sensitive adhesive film is probably the most innovative mounting aid available. It is a cellulose sheet sandwiched between two sheets of heavy protective paper. One protective sheet is removed, exposing the adhesive, and applied to the unit to be mounted. Place the unit in mounting position and peel away the other protective sheet from beneath (in slipsheet manner) as the unit sticks to the surface. This is an excellent method for mounting large photos and art.

WAXING MACHINE

The waxing machine is also a helpful device. It is simple to use but, as with all materials and equipment, its usefulness depends on your needs. The waxing machine coats the back of the unit with a thin layer of wax and is used in the same manner as one-coat cement.

Cement thinner does not dissolve this wax, a factor which can make it troublesome to lift a unit once it has been adhered into position. Try sliding your razor blade flatly along the edge and under it to remove the unit. Once lifted, it can be replaced without rewaxing. However, a unit that has been removed and replaced too often loses some of its tackiness, at least along the edges. This can give your work a messy look and can cause other problems as well. Almost anything can catch onto a loose edge and tear or remove the unit.

You'll find waxed proofs particularly useful in the preparation of book dummies. The use of wax for professional mechanicals is, however, debatable.

CHAPTER 2

TYPE AND ITS PREPARATION

Copy is usually created by the copywriter and presented to the art director in typewritten form. The art director must adapt this information to type according to particular specifications, in order to fit the layout.

Basically mathematical, converting copy into type is not complex in itself, but it can be perplexing to the beginner. On the other hand, the *use* of type has many esthetic functions in a design. This text will not deal with that aspect, but with the procedure for having type set.

Before you can control the esthetic use of type, you should know the many characteristics of type as a material. There are basically three methods of setting type: hand, machine, and phototypesetting.

HAND-SET TYPE
Each character—capital or lower case letters, numerals, punctuation marks, and symbols—is an engraved form set on a piece of metal called a *slug* (Fig. 37).

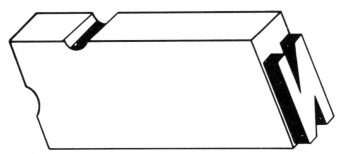

Fig. 37 Each character is engraved on a piece of metal called a slug.

Setting type by hand, the oldest method of all, is done by placing individual slugs into a composing stick, spelling out the copy one character at a time. After the type is set, it is placed into a form, inked with a roller, and printed onto a sheet of paper called a *type proof*. At the completion of proofing, the individual slugs are disassembled and returned to their respective cubicles (cases). This method of typesetting is usually confined to small amounts of type, such as headlines, captions, etc. Setting larger amounts of type, such as text, by hand could be very expensive and is usually done by machine or photographic methods of setting. Although hand-set type is still used for setting headlines, it is almost a thing of the past—having been replaced by phototypesetting.

MACHINE-SET TYPE
There are three kinds of machine equipment used for setting type: Linotype, Monotype, and Ludlow. Although each machine's principle is different, the result is a complete line of type molded into one long lead slug. Each slug is then grouped to form the text and printed onto proof paper.

Of the three machine methods, only Linotype seems to be surviving the type revolution. Although it is now less prevalent than phototypesetting, it is still a reasonably fast and economical method of having type set. However, "hot metal" (another name for Linotype) has its limitations: There are very few faces available in sizes large enough to accommodate headlines. Therefore, it is used primarily for text setting.

PHOTOTYPE
Since the birth of phototypesetting, it seems that every few months a new method is invented. Photocomposition has become so sophisticated that there is literally no limitation to possible type sizes. Hundreds of type faces, new and old, are available for headlines and text.

Phototype is precisely what the name describes. It is copy (type) photographically printed (set) one character at a time on photographic paper. It is clean, without irregularities, and it can be set as tight or as open as you may need. While phototype can sometimes be more expensive than hot metal, its quality is far superior.

TYPE TERMINOLOGY
Each letter in the alphabet should be referred to as a *character*. Capitals are called caps or upper case. The small characters are called lower case, consisting of an upper stroke called the *ascender* (as in the letter *b*) and a downward stroke called the *descender* (as in the letter *y*).

The design of a particular alphabet is called *face* or *style*, such as *Helvetica, Caslon, Futura,* etc. Type styles can be designed in *roman* (vertical strokes) or in *italics* (slanted strokes). The characters can be designed as simple strokes called *sans serif*, or with crosslines at the end of the main stroke called the *serif*.

Type styles offer a variety of proportions and weights, such as in the type face Futura. Futura looks like this—**NORMAL**—but it is also available in a narrower style called **CONDENSED**. Some faces are designed in a series of wider proportions called extended, such as EUROSTILE EUROSTILE EXTENDED, etc.

Many faces are also designed in various weights such as LIGHT, **MEDIUM** and **BOLD**

The size of type is measured from the top of an ascender to the bottom of the descender in a given alphabet. The scale of measure for type is not calculated in inches or fractions of an inch but in *points*. The inch has been broken down to approximately 72 points; e.g., ½″ would be 36 points, ¼″ would be 18 points. This method affords much more accurate measurements in minute increments.

The length of a line is measured in *picas* (6 picas to 1 inch). The pica is also broken down into points (12 points to 1 pica).

The better typographers offer a catalog of their available faces in what is called a type specimen book. The book is usually divided into sections of text faces and headline faces, according to the different typesetting systems used (perhaps including Linotype faces). Each page lists the name of the type face and shows the alphabet in caps, lower case, and numerals in the various sizes offered. Phototype text offers a much broader range of sizes, anywhere from 4 point type up to 32 or 36 point.

Linotype, on the other hand, is limited to 6 point to 14 or perhaps 18 point. The display or headline faces literally have no limit to their size (Figs. 40 and 43).

Fig. 38 illustrates a simple layout consisting of a headline and text. Fig. 39 is the typewritten copy to be converted into type to fit the layout.

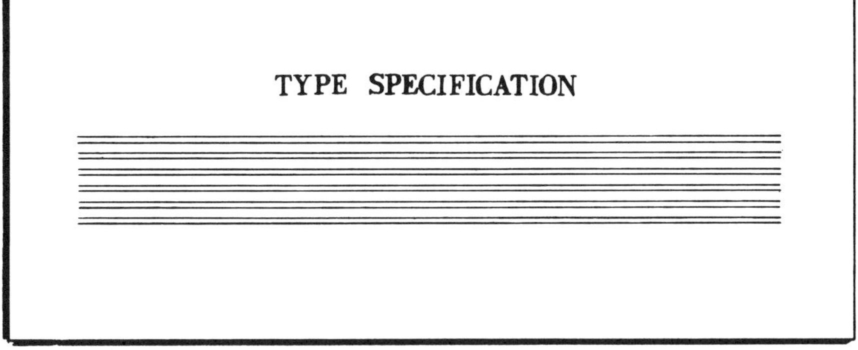

TYPE SPECIFICATION

Fig. 38 The layout: headline and text.

```
          TYPE SPECIFICATION

    Type is measured in points and picas.  There are

    72 points in one inch, 12 points in one pica, and

    6 picas in one inch.  Overall lengths and widths are

    usually calculated in picas, whereas the height

    of a character and the space between lines are measured

    in points.  When type is set "solid" it means normal

    spacing between lines.  If a block of copy needs to be

    made deeper it can be accomplished by opening the

    spaces between lines and inserting a required-size

    lead slug between each line.  This is called "leading"

    (pronounced "ledding") and is referred to as "1 point

    lead," "2 point lead," etc.
```

Fig. 39 The typewritten copy to be converted to type in the style indicated by the layout.

SPECIFYING TYPE: STEP ONE

After choosing the type face (Fig. 40), decide upon the size of the face you feel will fit the area indicated in the layout, which will also produce the same look or color to the line. Color, in this instance, means the value of gray the line presents. For example, observe the color of this page of text compared with the captions or a page from another textbook.

Suppose you decide on 18 point Bodoni for the headline. Count the characters in the headline in Fig. 38 (also count each space between words and each punctuation mark as a character). The count for this headline is 18 characters.

STEP TWO

Count 18 characters of 18 point Bodoni caps in the type book and measure the length with a pair of dividers or with a ruler. This represents an approximate length the line of type would be if you set it in that face at that size.

STEP THREE

Compare this measurement with the layout. If it is the correct length, you have chosen the correct size. If it is too short, count out the length in the next larger size. If it is too long, count out the length in the next smaller

BODONI REGULAR

HAND SET

10 POINT
AHIJKLMNOPQRSTUVWXYZABCDEFGHIJKLMNOPQ
abcdefghijklmnopqrstuvwxyz $1234567890

18 POINT
ARSTUVWXYZABCDEFGHIJKLM
abcdefghijklmnopqrstuv $12345678

24 POINT
ANOPQRSTUVWXYZABC
awxyzabcdefghijkl $901234

30 POINT
ADEFG amnopq $5678

36 POINT
AHIJK arstuvw $901

42 POINT
ALMN axyza $23

48 POINT
AOPQ abcd $45

60 POINT
ARS aefg $6

72 POINT
ATU ahij $

Fig. 40 Bodoni has been chosen as the type face.
This is how it might look in a specimen book.

27

size. Repeat this method for each point size illustrated on the page, until it measures the required length.

For the most part, absolute accuracy in setting text is virtually impossible. Should your closest calculation be only half a character or so too *short*, you can use that size, instructing the typographer to *open* the line to fit the measure needed. *Open* means to place space between each character and/or word to make the line longer. If no extra space is needed in a setting, it is referred to as set solid.

If your closest calculation shows the line to be too long by one character or so (and you are setting in Linotype), the typographer cannot help you. Metal type cannot be *closed*. You may have to compromise and set the line in a smaller size, or perhaps set it and have a photostat made to the required length—or use a face in the phototype section. Phototype text can be "closed" or *tightened* by bringing the characters closer together. This is called *kerning*.

In the event that you cannot ascertain a compromising size, choose another type face and start over. Once you have made the final decision on face and size, write instructions on the copy sheet (Fig. 41).

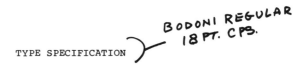

TYPE SPECIFICATION

Type is measured in points and picas. There are

72 points in one inch, 12 points in one pica, and

6 picas in one inch. Overall lengths and widths are

usually calculated in picas, whereas the height

of a character and the space between lines are measured

in points. When type is set "solid" it means normal

spacing between lines. If a block of copy needs to be

made deeper it can be accomplished by opening the

spaces between lines and inserting a required-size

lead slug between each line. This is called "leading"

(pronounced "ledding") and is referred to as "1 point

lead," "2 point lead," etc.

Fig. 41 Write instructions for the headline on the copy.

STEP FOUR

Count the characters in the typewritten copy. There are several approaches to doing this, but for the purpose of simplification, we will outline a standard procedure. Once this method is understood, you can develop your own.

The purpose of this count is to determine the approximate total number of characters in the entire block of copy. For example, if you had a shape measuring 47″ by 11″ and needed to know the square inch area of the space, you would multiply 47″ × 11″ and conclude 517 square inches to be the total area. Using the same formula to determine the total characters in this text, you must first determine the total characters in one line. Because the length of each line is irregular, establish an average length. Draw a vertical line through the copy to approximate an average length (Fig. 42).

Count the characters in one line up to this vertical line (each space between words and each punctuation mark are counted as one character). Although the text consists of caps and lower case, all is considered to be lower case in this instance. The count for the first line here would be 47 characters.

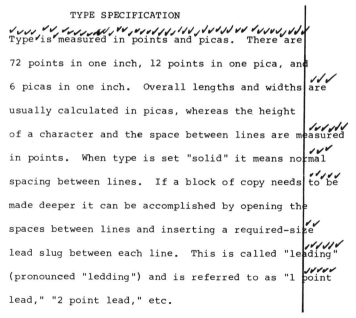

Fig. 42 Count the copy by establishing an average line and adding or deducting the characters that do not meet this average.

Count the number of lines in the text (11) and multiply 47 × 11. Your answer will be 517. Now count the characters to the right of the vertical line. Don't forget the space at the end of each line: 57 characters.

Add 517 and 57. Answer: 574 total characters. You must realize that this is an approximation. Each character—capital, lower case, punctuation mark, and numeral—is in a different proportion. An absolute count is impossible. The count is based on the use of the lower case *x* as an average character. Presumably, if the copy were set using all *x*'s there should be approximately 574. Even this is improbable, which means no one can be positive of any text count. Therefore, you are working with an assumed total.

Nevertheless, the system works quite well when understood, but you must remember that your calculations are flexible. The count could be off as much as 5 or 6 characters in either direction.

STEP FIVE

Measure the width of the text area decided in the layout: 4½" (or 27 picas). At this point, you should choose an appropriate point size if you haven't already. Let's try 8 point.

Note the line of copy above the upper right-hand corner of the sample copy (Fig. 43). It reads "characters per inch: lower case 18, caps 12." This is an average character count for you to work with. Not all type books illustrate their count in this fashion. Some have counts broken down in picas in the front or back of the book under various type face listings; some have pull-out sheets with counts for each face and size, etc. There are several ways in which typographers offer these calculations.

You are working with lower case and there are 18 characters to 1 inch. The layout is 4½" wide. Multiply 4.5 × 18. The answer, 81, indicates that there will be that many characters in 1 line if set in 8 point Bodoni. Most type showings offer the count in picas rather than inches. For example, the same specifications here would be 3 characters in 1 pica, and the layout is 27 picas wide. Multiply 27 picas × 3 characters. The answer is the same (81).

STEP SIX

If 81 characters will be used to fill 1 line, the remaining question is, "How many lines of copy will 574 characters occupy?" Divide 81 into 574. Answer: 7 lines with 6 characters left over. The 7 lines mean 7 complete lines. The 6 extra characters should be disregarded. Therefore, the type will occupy 7 lines of depth.

STEP SEVEN

You know how *wide* the copy will be because you have already determined that, but now you need to know how *deep* it will be.

BODONI REGULAR with ITALIC and SMALL CAPS
LINOTYPE

6 POINT Characters per inch: Lower Case 23, Caps 15

THE BEST AND THE MOST DURABLE FASHIONS QUICKLY BECOME DATED W
The best and the most durable fashions quickly become dated whenever styles change. T
THE BEST AND THE MOST DURABLE FASHIONS QUICKLY BECOME DATED W
The best and the most durable fashions quickly become dated whenever styles change. T
ABCDEFGHIJKLMNOPQRSTUVWXYZ $1234567890

8 POINT Characters per inch: Lower Case 18, Caps 12

THE BEST AND THE MOST DURABLE FASHIONS QUICKLY B
The best and the most durable fashions quickly become dated whenev
THE BEST AND THE MOST DURABLE FASHIONS QUICKLY B
The best and the most durable fashions quickly become dated whenev
ABCDEFGHIJKLMNOPQRSTUVWXYZ $1234567890

9 POINT Characters per inch: Lower Case 17, Caps 12

THE BEST AND THE MOST DURABLE FASHIONS QUICK
The best and the most durable fashions quickly become dated w
THE BEST AND THE MOST DURABLE FASHIONS QUICK
The best and the most durable fashions quickly become dated w
ABCDEFGHIJKLMNOPQRSTUVWXYZ $1234567890

10 POINT Characters per inch: Lower Case 15.5, Caps 10

THE BEST AND THE MOST DURABLE FASHIONS QU
The best and the most durable fashions quickly become da
THE BEST AND THE MOST DURABLE FASHIONS QU
The best and the most durable fashions quickly become da
ABCDEFGHIJKLMNOPQRSTUVWXYZ $1234567890

11 POINT Characters per inch: Lower Case 14.5, Caps 9

THE BEST AND THE MOST DURABLE FASHIONS
The best and the most durable fashions quickly become
THE BEST AND THE MOST DURABLE FASHIONS
The best and the most durable fashions quickly become
ABCDEFGHIJKLMNOPQRSTUVWXYZ $1234567890

12 POINT Characters per inch: Lower Case 14, Caps 9

THE BEST AND THE MOST DURABLE FASHIO
The best and the most durable fashions quickly beco
THE BEST AND THE MOST DURABLE FASHIO
The best and the most durable fashions quickly beco
ABCDEFGHIJKLMNOPQRSTUVWXYZ $1234567890

14 POINT Characters per inch: Lower Case 12.5, Caps 8

THE BEST AND THE MOST DURABLE FA
The best and the most durable fashions quickly
THE BEST AND THE MOST DURABLE FA
The best and the most durable fashions quickly
ABCDEFGHIJKLMNOPQRSTUVWXYZ $1234567890

Fig. 43 Note the character count that is given with the type face.

If your calculations indicate 7 lines of depth and you are using 8 point (height) type, multiply 8 point × 7 lines. Answer: 56 points. The text will be 56 points or approximately 4½ picas deep, which can be found on your pica rule in picas or points.

There are several "gauges" available which are an enormous aid in spacing type. For example, see Fig. 44. Here is how such a gauge is used. After determining the amount of lines (step six), you place the gauge over the layout, align the top mark in the 8 point slot with the top of the text area, and count down 7 lines; that is how deep 7 lines of 8 point type will be (Fig. 45). Simple?

So much for the mathematics of type specification. Needless to say, you will have to review these steps several times before you get the feel of it. Now let's carry the subject just a bit further. Suppose the 7 lines of depth is *not quite deep enough* to fill the area as in the layout. You have one of several decisions to make. Repeat the procedure, using a larger size, say 10 point, or try a different type face in the same size, or change the layout, or perhaps have the typographer open the space between each line to fit the depth (leading).

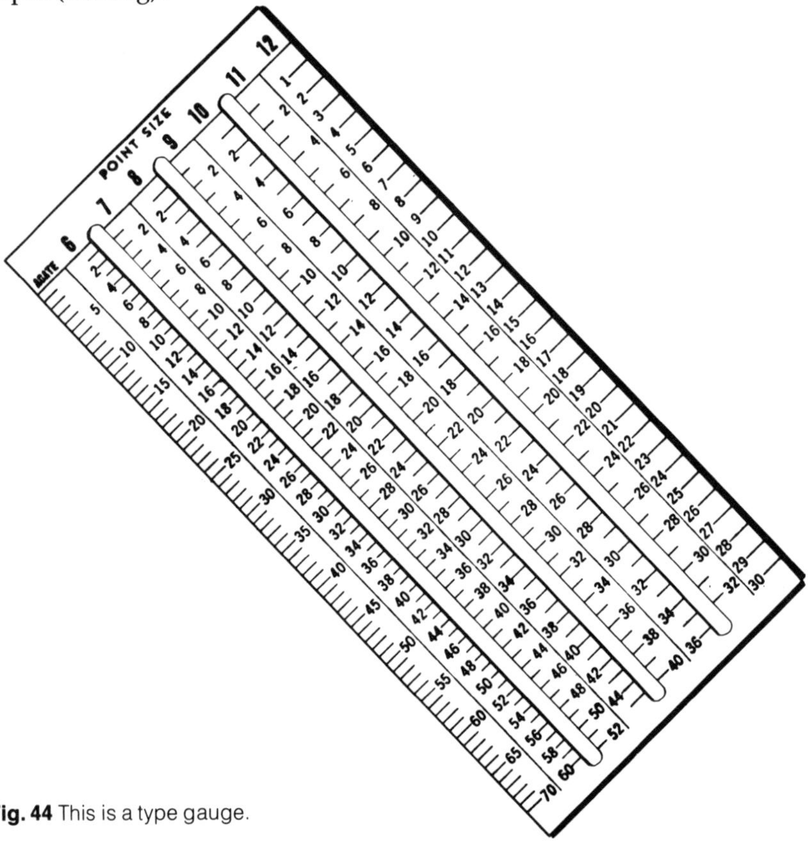

Fig. 44 This is a type gauge.

Leading between lines is usually done in points. For example, 2 points of lead between each line would be a possible leading. If 2 point leading is your decision, when using the scale you would not read the 8 point slot, but the 10 point slot (8 point + 2 point lead), down to 7. This gives approximately 2 points of lead between each line.

If you discover 7 lines of 8 point type to be *too deep* for the layout, you *cannot take space out*, because these calculations are based on setting the type *solid* (butting each line of metal), so that they cannot be placed any closer. You can possibly try a smaller size, another type face, or you can change the layout. If you are using phototype text, you have the capability to tighten or open the space between lines, since the type is moved photographically and there are no metal slugs that set physical boundaries.

The block of copy you worked with in this exercise is to be set *flush left* and *flush right*; i.e., the length of each line is the same. If your layout looked like Fig. 46, it would be called *flush left–rag* (ragged) *right*. In Fig. 47 it would be called *flush right–rag left*. Fig. 48 is *rag left and right*. Fig. 49 shows *centered lines*.

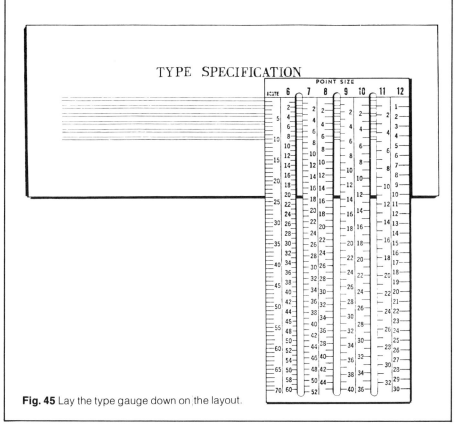

Fig. 45 Lay the type gauge down on the layout.

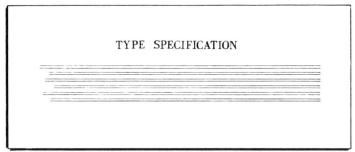

Fig. 46 Flush left, ragged right.

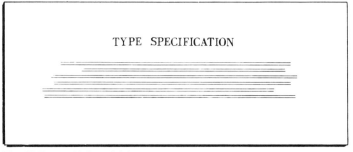

Fig. 47 Flush right, ragged left.

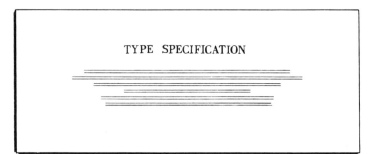

Fig. 48 Ragged left and right.

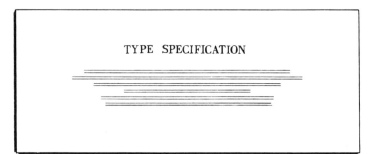

Fig. 49 Centered lines.

TYPE SPECIFICATION

Type is measured in points and picas. There are 72 points in one inch, 12 points in one pica, and 6 picas in one inch. Overall lengths and widths are usually calculated in picas, whereas the height of a character and the space between lines are measured in points. When type is set "solid" it means normal spacing between lines. If a block of copy needs to be made deeper it can be accomplished by opening the spaces between lines and inserting a required-size lead slug between each line. This is called "leading" (pronounced "ledding") and is referred to as "1 point lead," "2 point lead," etc.

Fig. 50 Type set solid.

TYPE SPECIFICATION

Type is measured in points and picas. There are 72 points in one inch, 12 points in one pica, and 6 picas in one inch. Overall lengths and widths are usually calculated in picas, whereas the height of a character and the space between lines are measured in points. When type is set "solid" it means normal spacing between lines. If a block of copy needs to be made deeper it can be accomplished by opening the spaces between lines and inserting a required-size lead slug between each line. This is called "leading" (pronounced "ledding") and is referred to as "1 point lead," "2 point lead," etc.

Fig. 51 Type set with 2 point lead.

At the conclusion of your calculations, you must legibly write out the instructions to the typographer. I cannot overemphasize the importance of legibility and neatness in writing your specifications. Avoid using *ink* for this; you may have to make changes. Your specs for this job, if set solid, would result in Fig. 50.

If set with 2 point lead: 8/10 point Bodoni 27 picas wide, caps and lower case, flush left and right (Fig. 51).

HANDLING TYPE PROOFS

If the setting is Linotype, the type proof should be handled with great care. When freshly printed, it will smear at the slightest touch. Therefore it should be "fixed" before using. To use a fixative spray, simply follow the directions on the can. However, be careful not to apply it too heavily, or it may blur the type and become very tacky. Be sure to use the Krylon "Crystal Clear" spray—not the "workable" fixative. The workable will make the ink run and turn it purple.

If you should be allergic to the spray fixative, you might try an old method: using ordinary white talcum powder. Just sprinkle it lightly onto the proof and spread it gently with cotton. At the completion of your paste-up, wipe the surface gently with clean cotton or soft tissue.

All this spraying and fixing is completely unnecessary when using phototype. It will not smear, nor can it be damaged by cement or thinner.

Examine the type proof thoroughly for broken or marred letters, which often appear. It is your job to repair the type with poster paint or India ink. A technical pen or fine crowquill may be useful for this.

Along with the type proof a "glassine," or "onionskin," proof is printed. An almost transparent paper, it is especially useful in checking the type against the layout for proper size and position.

Once the proof has been fixed, cement the back and allow it to dry. Place the proof back down onto a clean cardboard. (The back of a pad is useful here.) Then, with a razor blade, either cut out all the type to be used, or cut as you need it. Scissors also may be used.

PHOTOTYPESETTING

Because phototype can be enlarged to any size without irregularities or broken edges, it is very handy for the designer. In addition to this, photocomposition offers unlimited possibilities in design and arrangement of type. The characters can be tilted, curved, squashed, extended, reduced, and enlarged. They can be overlapped, made in perspective, and distorted. You will find phototype extremely useful in designing book jackets, album covers, brochures, presentations, 35 mm slides, or anything requiring large type or unusual arrangements of type. Phototypesetting also offers solutions for difficult shapes and sizes in body copy (text). There is no restriction in point size. For example, hot metal offers very specific sizes for each face: 6, 7, 8, 9, 10, 11 point, etc. But with phototype, you can set 9½ point, 11¾ point, or whatever size is required. It is set to fit.

When ordering phototype, supply the typographer with a fairly accurate layout, proper typewritten copy, the type face desired, and the approximate point size. It will all be set in position to proper size and arrangement. Simple, from the art director's point of view, but not inexpensive.

POSITIONING TYPE

Various procedures for aligning type may be employed. One method is to line up the bottom of the type with a T-square, then with a blue pencil lightly draw a line at either extreme of the type, both horizontally and vertically, signifying a corner. Corresponding lines should be drawn on the board (mechanical) in the desired position. Apply cement to the board and allow it to dry, or, while it is still wet, position the type, matching the lines on the proof with those on the mechanical (Fig. 52). Tweezers or razor blades are used to manipulate type. With the corner of a razor blade or with tweezers "tack" the type down into position. Then check for squareness with a T-square.

For faster results, just draw a horizontal and a vertical line on the board, indicating one corner where your type is to be positioned, and line up your type directly on the board with a T-square and triangle, adjusting

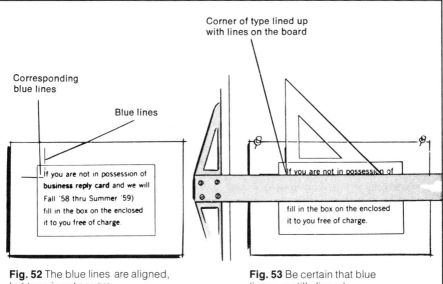

Fig. 52 The blue lines are aligned, but type is not square.

Fig. 53 Be certain that blue lines are still aligned.

with forefinger and thumb, tweezers, or any suitable device for manipulation (Fig. 53).

A quicker way is to place the type visually in the approximate position and, using your dividers to calculate the actual position, adjust the type. For the beginner, this last method may be too tricky. At the start, it would be best to use one of the other methods. You will gradually develop your own system.

If you should use the dry cement method of pasting large areas of type (with two-coat cement), slipsheets placed under the type proof will be very convenient. If, while mounting type, the cement should be too tacky, preventing freedom of manipulation, you may apply thinner to dissolve the cement, thus permitting easier shifting of type. If you do this, wait until the cement has dried beneath the proof before pressing it firmly into position, or it may slide out of square. Wet cement may also squeeze out and over the type, causing it to smear.

Probably the best approach for positioning type is to use the glassine. Simply place the glassine type proof (see page 36) over the layout, lining up the copy properly. Mark off the corners of the ad, or make any other suitable key marks for registration. Then position the glassine in the identical position, using the corresponding registration marks on the mechanical. Tape the glassine down at the top. Lift the glassine with one hand and slide the type proof beneath it with the other. After matching the type proof with the glassine, lift the glassine and adjust the type proof for squareness and accuracy of position with a T-square. Then press firmly.

Where a glassine cannot be used (such as with art, photos, shapes, etc.), the layout, if on transparent (tracing or visual bond) paper, may be taped into position onto the mechanical. Follow the same procedure as in the use of the glassine. Simply lift the layout, place the piece to be mounted beneath it, and line it up with the indication on the layout. If the layout is not on transparent paper, you may make a fairly accurate tracing of the overall size of each element in the layout and follow the same procedure.

Centering type or any element is not always done mechanically, for the simple reason that a line of type (although perfectly centered within an area) may appear to be off-center. This is rectified by raising the line slightly above center until it is optically centered. As long as the element *looks* centered, according to your judgment, it should be sufficient, except in cases when an element must be mechanically centered because of production or technical reasons. However, in most jobs, this optical centering should be sufficient.

TRANSFER TYPE

Transfer or rub-off sheets are especially useful in preparing dummies, layouts, and presentations; if used with care, they can be used for reproduction. The type character or numeral is printed on a wax-backed, thin acetate film. When the film is placed, waxed side down, onto a surface, burnished, and lifted, the character is transferred from the sheet to the surface. By using the printed guide lines with each character, several can be aligned to produce a word or words. They are available in several sizes and faces in black or color. Prestype type sheets are also useful. The type is not transferred from these but is simply burnished in position and then cut out.

RESPACING TYPE

After it is set, type does not always fit the space indicated in the layout. Because of this, some compensation must be made. Perhaps a photostat (which will be explained later) of the type reduced or enlarged will solve the problem. But more than likely, if you "open up" or "close up" the space between the lines ("line-spacing"), it will fit. In addition to adjusting the space between the lines, you may have to open or close up the space between the words ("word-spacing") or between the letters ("letter-spacing").

The following system may be used in line-spacing type to fit another size or shape. First, cement the proof into the approximate position. Then, with a razor blade and a steel T-square, cut between each line (Fig. 54). Wet this down with thinner and slide each line (with the corner of a razor blade or tweezers) away from the others, opening the spaces between them until the desired size has been reached (Fig. 55). Be certain

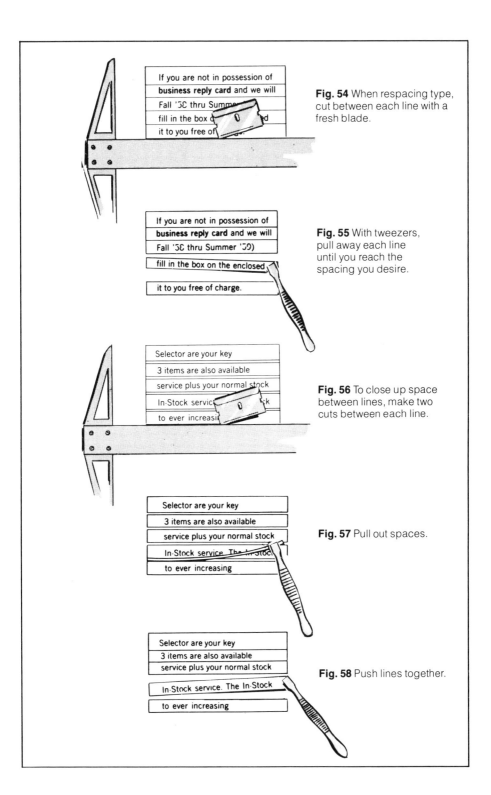

If you are not in possession of
business reply card and we will
Fall '5C thru Summer
fill in the box
it to you free of

Fig. 54 When respacing type, cut between each line with a fresh blade.

If you are not in possession of
business reply card and we will
Fall '5C thru Summer '50)
fill in the box on the enclosed
it to you free of charge.

Fig. 55 With tweezers, pull away each line until you reach the spacing you desire.

Selector are your key
3 items are also available
service plus your normal stock
In-Stock servic
to ever increasi

Fig. 56 To close up space between lines, make two cuts between each line.

Selector are your key
3 items are also available
service plus your normal stock
In-Stock service The
to ever increasing

Fig. 57 Pull out spaces.

Selector are your key
3 items are also available
service plus your normal stock
In-Stock service. The In-Stock
to ever increasing

Fig. 58 Push lines together.

that the space between each line is the same. Use your dividers as a guide.

To close up the space, make two cuts between each line, wet down the area with thinner, and pull out the space. (Note: thinner will not affect the type.) Then push each line closer (Figs. 56, 57, and 58).

If word-spacing or letter-spacing is required, use the same method as in line-spacing. The only difference is that the cut marks are made between the letters or words, and you either push them together or pull them apart, being certain that they are kept "square" with your T-square and triangle (Figs. 59 and 60).

Cutting directly on the mechanical is sometimes frowned upon by the art director. It does leave unsightly cut marks on the mechanical if done carelessly or if an element must be moved after cutting. Nevertheless, it is a very accurate and convenient method.

Of course, there are other ways to achieve the same results. After having cemented the back of the type proof, you might cut each line separately on a cutting board and place each one individually on the mechanical, adjusting them until the required size is attained.

Some artists do their respacing on a separate piece of two-ply Strathmore or bond paper, then cut the new arrangement out as a unit and place it in position on the mechanical. This method avoids cut marks on the mechanical; in the event that the block of type has to be shifted or repositioned, this can be done without having to respace the type again.

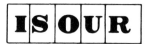

Fig. 59 To letter-space, cut apart each letter freehand.

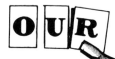

Fig. 60 Pull apart the letters, without letting the tweezers touch the type.

CURVING TYPE

Although type can be curved photomechanically, it is possible that time and budget may not permit this approach, in which case it must be done on the mechanical. No matter where you work, you will inevitably have to curve type at one time or another. There are two excellent methods of doing this.

Fig. 61 shows a rough layout of a line of curved type. Fig. 62 is the type as it is printed (proof). Place a sheet of tracing paper over the layout and make a very accurate pencil line of the desired curve, along either the bottom or the top edge of the type. Use a French curve and a 6H pencil.

Indicate the beginning and end of the line of type. Tape this tracing over a sheet of two-ply Strathmore (Fig. 63). Lift the tissue back. Coat the paper with rubber cement and allow it to dry. Cement the back of the type proof and allow it to dry.

If you use one-coat cement, coat only the back of the type proof and allow it to dry.

At this stage, you can curve your type using one of two methods. The first one is as follows. Place the cemented type face up onto a clean cutting board, then cut away the excess paper around it to facilitate handling. Do not cut closer than $\frac{1}{16}$" or so. Carefully box cut around each character with a razor blade (or one character at a time as needed), as shown in Fig. 64.

Bring the tissue back over the cemented paper. Holding it at the bottom with your left hand, raise it slightly from the surface. Lift the first character from the type proof with your tweezers and position it under the tracing. Very carefully, line up the character with the pencil indication on the tissue. Anchor it into position by pressing the corner of the piece with your tweezers. When manipulating in this manner, be careful not to mar the type.

Repeat the same procedure with the last character (Fig. 65). You now have the limits set for the length of the line. Work between them. Now, *roughly*, position each character in the same manner, controlling the space between them optically (Fig. 66). Do not press them down at this stage. It is too soon to set them permanently.

If you work carefully, simply resting each letter on the paper, it will be easier to manipulate them. Once you have pressed it, the cement will grip, making it difficult to move the pieces. This takes a bit of practice, but if your cement is mixed to the proper consistency, you can actually lift and reposition the pieces without having to wet them down with thinner, in the beginning at least.

After you have roughly positioned all the pieces beneath the tissue, lift the tissue back and continue manipulating further. If pieces become difficult to move, wet them with thinner. *Do not flood the paper*. Just a slight squirt of thinner will be sufficient. Some artists apply thinner with a small brush or an eye dropper.

Now bring the tissue down in place and check the type for proper curve. Lift the tissue and adjust the type further if needed. Once again, bring the tissue down over the assembly and check it. Lift the tissue and adjust; bring the tissue down and check; lift the tissue and adjust. Repeat this until you have all the characters lined up properly and readably spaced.

Do not burnish into position while the cement is wet or the pieces will shift. Lift the tissue and allow the cement to dry around and beneath the pieces. When dry, place a piece of tissue over the assembly and burnish into position firmly.

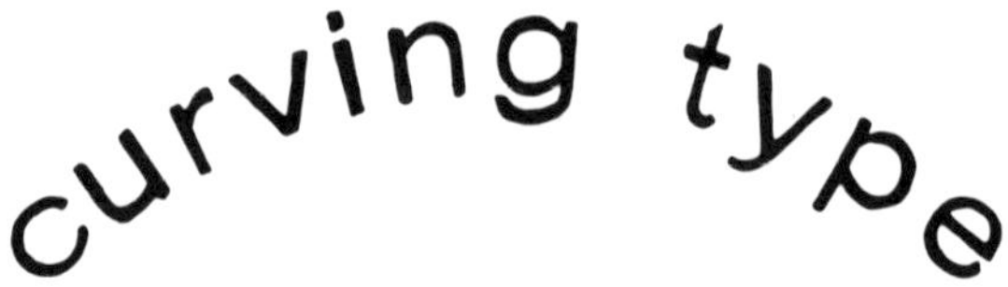

curving type

Fig. 61 A rough layout of a line of curved type.

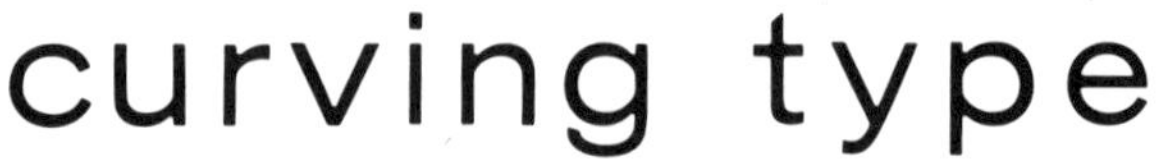

curving type

Fig. 62 The type has been set in a straight line.

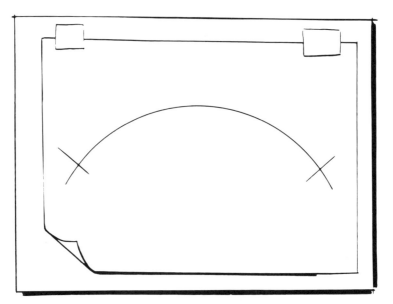

Fig. 63 Tape the tracing paper—indicating the desired curve—over a board.

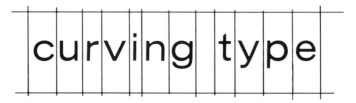

Fig. 64 Cut above, below, and between each printed letter.

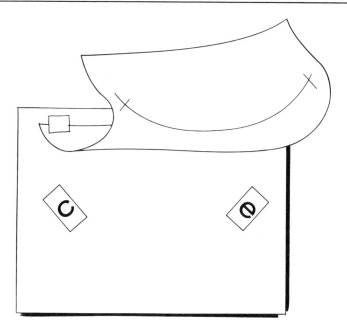

Fig. 65 Position first and last characters, using the tissue overlay as a guide.

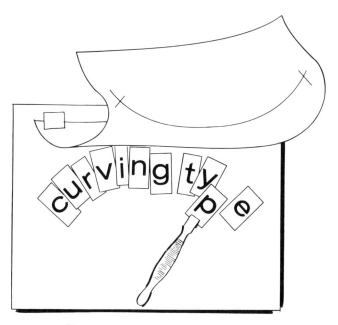

Fig. 66 Position each letter roughly.

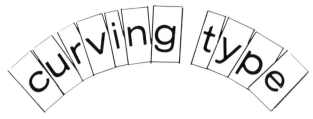

Fig. 67 After you have cleaned around the type, the result should look like this.

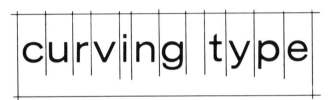

Fig. 68A The second method of curving type: cut between each letter from the top to just below the bottom edge.

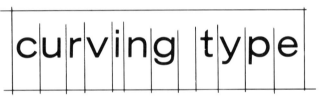

Fig. 68B Or you can cut from below to nearly the top edge, if you are curving type in the opposite direction.

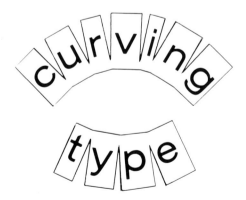

Fig. 69 The result of the second method of curving type: type is fanned out to the curve.

Make a final check with the tissue to be certain that the pieces did not shift. The cut marks around the characters often deceive your judgment in spacing. If you look at the type through your tracing paper (pulled slightly away from the surface), these lines will become diffused, permitting a better impression of the placement of the characters.

Clean up the excess cement from around the pieces. This is where your nerves are put to the test. After you have spent twenty minutes manipulating these pieces into position, one or two may pull away while you pick up the rubber cement. This is especially true when working with small characters. Try pressing the flat end of your tweezers on each piece as you clean around it. This will help. If a piece repeatedly comes up, you can cement it in position again or use a white water-soluble glue instead of cement. You can also try a dab of white poster paint as a glue.

In many instances, a piece will overlap an adjoining piece after it has been curved. You will obviously have to cut it away with a razor blade. However, with small pieces, *do not use a cutting motion*; i.e., do not *pull* the blade across the piece. This may tear it or pull it out of position. Actually, it is best to position the blade where you want to cut and then *press*, rather than pull. The excess will snap away. The result should look like Fig. 67.

The second method for curving type is to follow the same preliminary procedures as before, to the point of cutting out each character. Now, rather than cut out each character, you can cut between each from the top to just below the bottom edge (Fig. 68A). Should the curve bend in the opposite direction, cut from the bottom to the top edge of each character (Fig. 68B).

Position the entire line beneath the tissue, aligning it with the curve. Then, lightly, wet the unit with thinner and bend the line according to the indication of the required curve. Each character will fan out. This takes a fair amount of manipulation and is a rather direct approach. However, the line has a tendency to buckle. Should it be too short for the full length of the curve, you will have to cut it apart anyway. The result should look like Fig. 69.

Wet cement invariably transfers to the underside of the tracing during the manipulation. Remove it from the tissue or it may stick to the characters and pull them away when you lift the tissue. Of course, if you are using "one-coat" cement, the entire procedure is less messy and perhaps faster. However, the use of either type of cement is a matter of personal choice.

CHAPTER 3

COMPONENTS OF THE MECHANICAL

A PRINTED ADVERTISEMENT cannot be produced without some sort of printing plate. The printing plate cannot be made without some sort of original composite of the elements involved. The mechanical is this original makeup, consisting of all the components in their respective positions precisely as they are to appear on the printed page. The printing plate is made directly from this mechanical (Figs. 70 and 71).

In order to prepare a mechanical properly, its "language" must be learned. Particular rules are observed to make the mechanical's requirements visually understandable to the cameraman, such as the use of crop marks, bleed, screen indications, etc. In this chapter, some of the basic components of the mechanical—particularly the handling of art work —will be discussed.

Even though the rules given here are a *must* in all mechanicals, the methods of execution may vary according to the agency or the platemaker with whom you will be working. This will be discussed more thoroughly later on.

PHOTOSTATS
One of the most serviceable facilities in assembling a paste-up or mechanical is the photostat. The basic difference between a photostat and a photograph is that the stat negative is opaque paper and the photo negative is transparent film. A photostat is much less expensive than a regular photograph, and both the negative and positive can be very useful. For instance, if the layout calls for white type on a black background (reversed copy), you will obtain the proper results by ordering a negative stat of the original black type (Figs. 72 and 73).

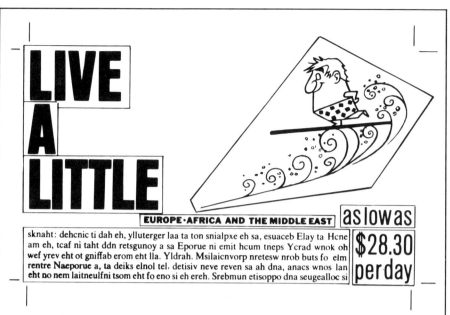

Fig. 70 All units are pasted up in this mechanical for an advertisement.

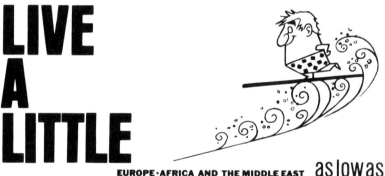

Fig. 71 No cut marks show on the printed page.

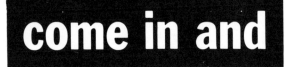

Fig. 72 A positive stat shows black type on a white background.

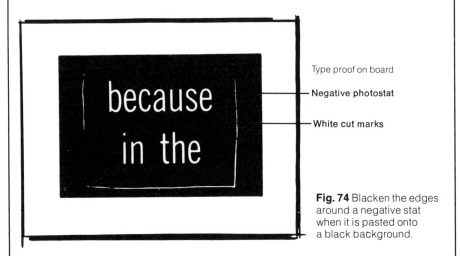

Fig. 73 A negative stat shows white type on a black background.

Type proof on board

Negative photostat

White cut marks

Fig. 74 Blacken the edges around a negative stat when it is pasted onto a black background.

Although there are various types of stat paper available, generally you will be concerned with two—the matte and the glossy. Matte stats hold, with limited accuracy, various gradations of tone values (similar to the photograph), while the glossy is confined to black and white with no intermediate values. (See Chapter 4.)

The stat has a variety of uses in paste-ups and mechanicals. For example, in assembling a dummy or layout where art work or photos are required, a stat is used instead in order to preserve the actual art or photo. In preparing a mechanical, the same procedure is followed, especially when the art is not actual reproduction size. A stat of the art, reduced or enlarged to the required size and placed in position on the mechanical, acts as a visual guide for size and position for the cameraman and platemaker to follow. It also shows the mechanical artist whether or not the art will fit in its proper position or if it meets the requirements of the layout.

Because the matte stat is not a true representation of the art in its proper tonal values, it is used just for the purpose of showing size and position of the art in the mechanical and under very few circumstances for reproduction.

The glossy stat, on the other hand, may be used for reproduction. Because of the sharpness of its black and white areas, it is very often used as a means of reducing or enlarging lettering, type, line drawings, etc., and can be properly positioned in the mechanical. However, a glossy stat of tone art, such as a photo or wash drawing, will break up and appear blotchy. Values of gray of less than 50% intensity will tend to bleach out, while those over 50% will tend to fill in, resulting in a very poor representation of the original art. Therefore, the art must have no values of gray if it is to produce a good, clean black and white line glossy photostat to be used for reproduction.

When a negative stat is cemented onto a black background, be certain to blacken the edges around the stat after cutting it out (see page 110). This will prevent paste-up and cut marks from appearing on the cameraman's negatives and will eliminate unnecessary work for the film stripper (Fig. 74).

Another advantage of the photostat is that, if necessary, a reverse position print of the art can be made. This is called "flopping" the art. It comes in handy if your art is facing one way and the layout calls for it to face the other way (Figs. 75 and 76).

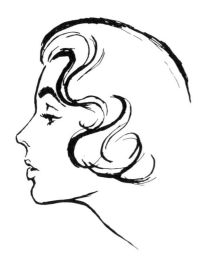 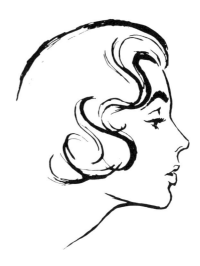

Fig. 75 Here is the original art.

Fig. 76 The original art has been flopped (not reversed) in the stat.

1 s/s glossy (or matte) neg. (or pos.)

Fig. 77 Here is how you indicate the art for a same size (s/s) photostat.

|←— 11" BM (between marks) —→|
1 glossy (or matte) neg. (and/or pos.)

Fig. 78 For a reduction or enlargement, indicate with two marks the extremes needed. Connect these marks with arrows and write instructions. This may be done on the back of the original copy, on a tissue taped over it, or in the margin.

|←— 4" BM —→|
This is pos., 1 glossy (or matte) neg.

Fig. 79 Frequently, the original copy seems to be a negative when actually it is a positive (or vice versa). In order to prevent confusion, you might indicate that the original art is negative or positive.

|←——— 4" BM —→|
1 glossy (or matte) 1st (and/or 2nd) print

Fig. 80 Another solution to this problem is to refer to the negative or positive as a first or second print. If you want the opposite impression of the original copy, ask for a first print. When the same impression is needed, ask for a second print.

1 glossy neg. (your measure of the orig. copy) ↑(enlarged to) 17"
1 glossy neg. 4" (reduced to) ↓ 2"

Fig. 81 The distance between the marks you indicate on the copy (Fig. 78) is measured at the stat house, and a percentage for the reduction or enlargement is worked out. To avoid error, you might write the measurements yourself.

For same size

1 glossy 1st print s/s

For reduction

1 glossy 1st print (and/or 2nd print) 4" ↓ 2"

For enlargement

1 glossy 1st print 4" ↑ 13"

Fig. 82 By giving full instructions, according to Figs. 80 and 81, you will avoid the possibility of error.

HOW TO ORDER PHOTOSTATS

Figs. 77 to 82 show several procedures employed in ordering stats. The method you choose depends entirely on the requirements of the original copy, the organization you work for, or the stat house being used.

For the sake of economy and time, it is advisable, when more than one piece is to be statted in the same proportion (focus), to assemble ("gang up") as many as possible on one board and have it statted as a unit. Subsequently, one print will contain all units for the cost of one.

When you want a particular portion of the original blown up (whether you use a photostat or photograph), be certain to indicate this on your order, on a tissue over the art, or on the back of the art. Simply circle or box in the area and write, "Take in just this area." Otherwise, the cameraman will have no way of knowing you need only a particular area and will naturally assume the entire piece of art is to be taken in. For example, Fig. 83 shows the art properly marked for the blow-up in Fig. 84. If the area desired had *not* been marked properly, the stat might have come back looking like Fig. 85. This is a common error that can be avoided with a little forethought. One is waste enough, but several at one time can be very exasperating.

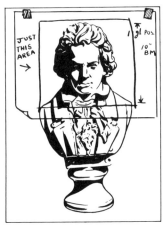

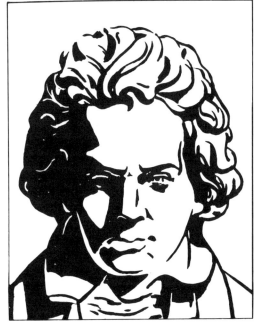

Fig. 83 Here is the original art properly marked for a blow-up. Be specific.

Fig. 84 Here is the art blown up (11″ × 14″).

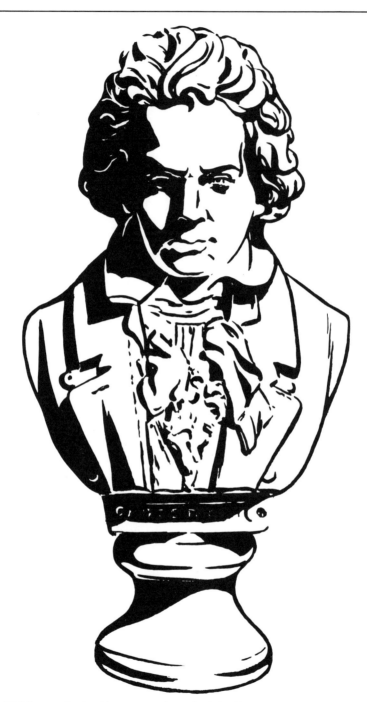

Fig. 85 If the area had *not* been properly marked, the blow-up would have looked like this (18″ × 24″).

DIRECT POSITIVE

The direct positive print is most useful and perhaps of better quality. This requires no negative, thus saving that cost and time.

BLEACHING STATS

You will find a bleaching kit very helpful in working with stats or photos in both finished art and for preparing dummies or presentations. For example, you can erase a line of type or area without having to blacken the negative or reshoot it. It is good for general clean-up if you prefer not to use white paint.

GHOSTED STATS

A device particularly useful in preparing line drawings is the ghosted photostat. A stat is made from your reference material grayed down (ghosted) to about 50% value, just enough to see the object in detail. You can then ink (use a waterproof ink) over the image directly on the photostat. Allow suitable drying time, then bleach over the entire photostat. The ghosted image will disappear, leaving your inked version as a black line drawing.

In preparing dummies, presentations of layouts that may call for stats of type, for example, to be painted over in another color, it would be much easier if you ordered the stats "ghosted." The paint will cover it with less trouble and will look much neater.

PERSPECTIVE STATS

The perspective stat is a helpful service. For difficult line drawings of items or products that have labels or involved shapes, you can send the actual item to the stat house and have it statted in the perspective you need. You can then trace or draw from the stat. If there is a label on the item and you want it reproduced, you can cut it out of the stat and paste it onto your drawing. Be certain it is sharp black and white. If it is not, touch it up. Type and art can also be shot in perspective.

When ordering a perspective shot, you *must* send along a sketch of the overall shape in the perspective you want. Sketch directly from the object; do not attempt to draw it from memory if you expect any degree of accuracy. Remember, the stat may not match the sketch perfectly, because statting in perspective is a difficult thing to accomplish and requires skill on the part of the cameraman. If you are going to use it only as a guide in preparing your finished art, you can make adjustments later. If possible, lucy the item (in outline) to the size and perspective you want. This will be much more accurate and closer to what the stat camera will see.

A lucy, incidentally, is a camera device for projecting an enlargement or reduction of art work or anything that can be placed flat in the machine. It projects the subject onto paper, or through tracing paper, enabling you to visualize effectively the art work in its new dimension. The lucy is useful for scaling photos, art, type, and layouts and is an enormous help to illustrators and designers.

Needless to say, photostats have many uses. If ever you are confronted with an unusual problem, there is a chance that it can be solved photostatically. The best thing to do is to call your stat house and present them with your problem. They may be able to solve it or at least offer a constructive suggestion.

DRAWING PERSPECTIVE
In illustrations (particularly industrial subjects) where an involved perspective calls for vanishing points beyond the capacity of your drawing table, you might try making your initial drawing a smaller, more convenient size, have it photostatted up to finished size, and trace it off. Or you can use your light box to trace it on the *back* of the stat (making revisions); then place the stat face up in position on the illustration board and rub it down, transferring the pencil drawing from the back of the stat to the illustration board. If you are working on a thin enough Strathmore, you will be able to trace the stat directly with the light box.

MARKING PHOTOGRAPHS
Photographs are frequently used in advertising. They are costly; therefore, proper handling is essential.

Never write on the surface or on the back of the photo with a hard pencil; the markings will crease the emulsion of the photo and perhaps mar it. If marking or writing is unavoidable, use a grease crayon on the front, on the back, or on a tissue taped over the photo. The grease crayon can be removed from the emulsion side with thinner and cotton. *Caution:* it may stain.

If you use felt-tip pens for marking photos, do so with discretion. The ink from felt-tip pens may be removed with thinner or perhaps with some soapy water or cotton, but be careful not to destroy the emulsion of the photo.

MOUNTING PHOTOS WITH A DRY MOUNT PRESS
A dry mount press (Fig. 86), also referred to as a *hot mount*, is a permanent and probably the best method of mounting photos. The press itself consists of an electrically heated metal plate that is pressed against the photo which has been placed over the mounting board. A sheet of "dry mount tissue"—a thin sheet, resembling heavy waxed paper—is placed between the back of the photo and the mounting board (Fig. 87). The tissue, having a dry adhesive on both sides, is heated by the electric plate, softening the adhesive. While the hot plate is forced against the mounting

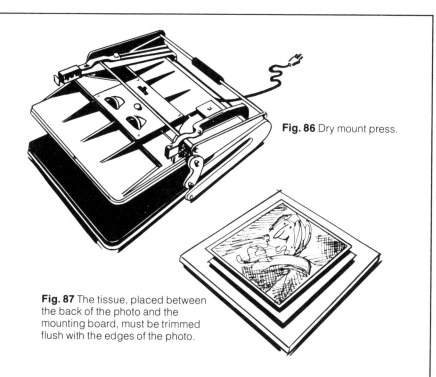

Fig. 86 Dry mount press.

Fig. 87 The tissue, placed between the back of the photo and the mounting board, must be trimmed flush with the edges of the photo.

surface, the heat forces the glue into the fiber of the back of the photo and the surface of the mounting board. When the heated plate is removed, the glue hardens, fusing the photo to the board. Once mounted, the photo cannot be removed.

MOUNTING PHOTOS WITHOUT A PRESS

For mounting a photograph securely when a dry mount press is not available, use double coats of "two-coat" cement on both surfaces and slipsheet them. If you use one-coat cement, the mount will not be as good if the cement is coated on only one surface. However, if you coat *both* surfaces, the mounting will be more permanent than with two-coat. Remember, you cannot slipsheet with one-coat cement. Allow both coated surfaces to dry, then very carefully mount the photo as shown in Figs. 201 and 202. But before mounting, be certain to check the back of the photo for names, key numbers, identification, etc. This information should be transferred to the back of the board upon which the photo is to be mounted. *Caution:* you will often find photos with slips of paper containing relevant data pasted on the back. This paper should be removed carefully and cemented onto the back of the board after mounting. If it is not removed, its impression will show up on the face of the photo.

When mounting a photograph, leave a wide margin around the photo (2" or more) for written production instructions and for protection of the edges. Mount onto a smooth, heavy stock—never use pebbled matboard. After mounting, place a sheet of bond paper over the photo and burnish flat with a straightedge.

A layout will frequently call for photos to be used smaller or larger than the original. In such cases, a photostat is made, bringing it down or up to the required size. This stat is placed in position on the mechanical and crossed out with a red pencil. The stat serves only as a guide for size and position. The original is mounted separately and sent along with the mechanical to the platemaker. The cameraman, upon shooting the negatives, will make a separate negative directly from the original photo (in the focus indicated by the stat) and combine ("strip in") the negatives accordingly.

SILHOUETTING
Quite often a layout will require a silhouetted photo in which the edges of the image are silhouetted. It is your job to white out the areas not needed in the photo. To begin with, the surface of the photo is often greasy, making it extremely difficult for paint to adhere. Several methods can be employed to overcome this. One of them is the use of "pounce," a powdery substance which can be sprinkled and rubbed over the emulsion and cleaned away with a dry tissue or handkerchief. This gives a slight "tooth" to the emulsion. However, be especially careful not to use it on "RC" (resin-coated) photo paper, as it will scratch the emulsion.

If you order a print that you know is to be silhouetted, instruct the photo lab to prepare it on "N" paper. This is an RC emulsion but with a "matte" finish that is more compatible with retouching techniques.

Another method of rendering a more sympathetic surface on the photo is the use of "non-crawl," which is mixed with the paint, giving it an adhesive quality. Saliva or thinner, rubbed on with cotton, often will serve the same purpose. The most desirable method depends upon the individual and his or her experience.

Using white paint and a good brush, start to silhouette by meticulously outlining the entire shape with a line about the weight of a heavy pencil line (Fig. 88). Then paint a border of white approximately ½" wide along this line (Fig. 89). The thin outline will act as a wall along the edge, which will enable you to flow the paint along it.

It is better to build up the paint with thin coats rather than to attempt complete coverage with a single thick layer. If it is too thick, the paint may crack and flake off.

At the completion of the silhouetting (and when the paint has thoroughly dried), place a sheet of medium-weight bond over the entire photo. Lightly trace a line along the center of the white border. Then place

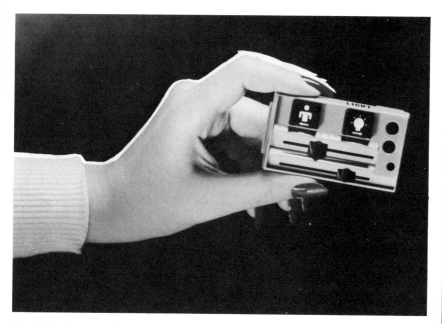

Fig. 88 To silhouette, first outline around the desired area with a heavy line of white paint.

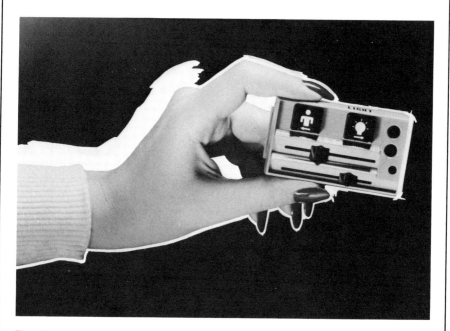

Fig. 89 Keeping the coverage uniform, apply a border of white paint approximately ½″ wide.

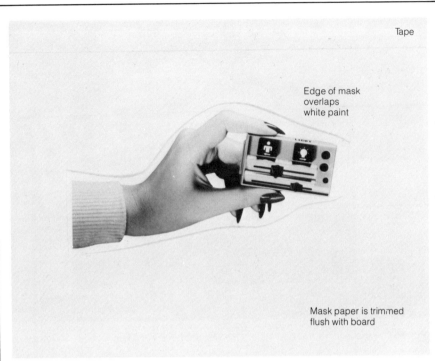

Tape

Edge of mask
overlaps
white paint

Mask paper is trimmed
flush with board

Fig. 90 Place a mask onto the photo in such a position that it overlaps the white without touching the silhouetted edge.

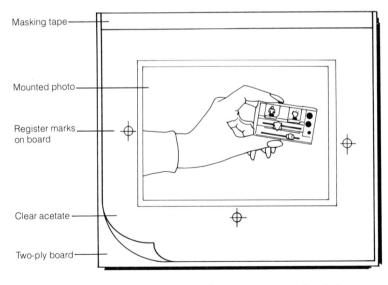

Masking tape

Mounted photo

Register marks
on board

Clear acetate

Two-ply board

Fig. 91A Tape a sheet of clear acetate over the photo.

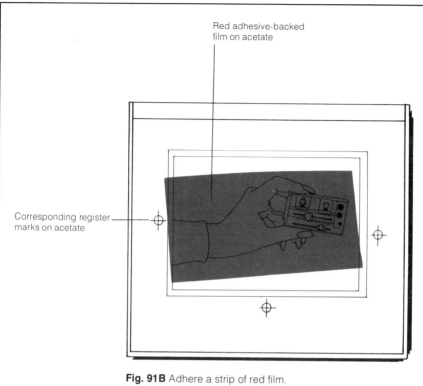

Red adhesive-backed
film on acetate

Corresponding register
marks on acetate

Fig. 91B Adhere a strip of red film.

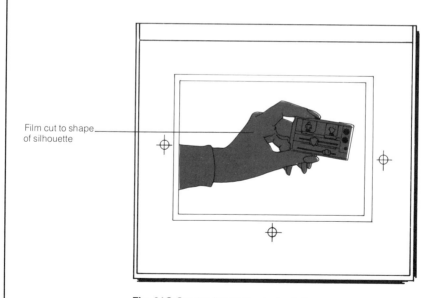

Film cut to shape
of silhouette

Fig. 91C Cut the film to the desired shape.

the bond onto a piece of cardboard and cut out the outlined area. Place this "mask" onto the photo in such a position as to overlap the white, but not to touch the silhouetted edge. This will automatically white out the remaining unwanted areas, without disturbing the silhouetted edge (Fig. 90). Then cut the top edge of the mask about ½" shorter than the board and secure this with a length of tape across the top. Turn the board over and trim off any excess paper. Write any needed information along the edge of the mask or on a tissue taped over it, being certain not to write over an area of the photo.

In the event that the silhouetted photo in its entirety is needed later, the paint may be washed off with cotton and water. *Caution:* the emulsion may bubble, peel, or tear if saturated or rubbed too hard. Never silhouette a photo before mounting it firmly onto heavy stock. If silhouetting is done before mounting, the photo will buckle and the paint will crack or flake off, making it difficult to mount the photo without damaging it.

If there is only one photo available and the layout indicates that the photo is to appear in one area in its entirety and silhouetted in another, the photo may be prepared in the following manner.

Mount the photo and key it to correspond with the mechanical. Then tape a sheet of frosted acetate or vellum over it and outline the silhouetted area with a thin red line (Fig. 91). This will enable the cameraman to shoot the complete photo and use the red outline as a guide in silhouetting (opaquing) the *negative* for the second shot.

Another faster and easier method is to cut a "mask" silhouette with masking film. If it isn't necessary to show the photo silhouetted to the client (or whomever), this is actually the most practical approach, since the photo is left intact.

Tape a sheet of clear acetate over the photo. Then strip a piece of 100% orange-red color film (see "Color Film Sheet," page 17) onto the acetate large enough to cover the subject to be silhouetted. Then carefully (lightly) cut the film, following the edge as you would with white paint. Peel away the outside excess. When finished you will have created a red shape *covering* the subject. When this overlay is photographed (separately) by the platemaker, it will be used to create the silhouetted plate.

Masking film is probably the best material for this kind of silhouetting. In the long run this last method is the most practical because the platemaker must cut a similar mask over your white paint silhouette in order to create a silhouette halftone plate. It is a misconception that the white paint in itself creates the silhouette halftone. This is not so. The white paint is recorded on the halftone negative as a fine dot and must be removed (see page 69).

CHAPTER 4

APPLIED METHODS OF THE MECHANICAL MAKEUP

T HERE ARE TWO TYPES of art: *line* and *continuous tone*. Line art, such as black and white line drawings, type, etc., contains no gray, that is, no intermediate values of black and white (Fig. 92).

Continuous tone art consists of a range of values from white through black: photo, wash drawing, oil painting, etc. (Fig. 93).

PHOTOENGRAVING FOR LETTERPRESS PRINTING

In order to reproduce the respective effects of line and continuous tone art, a metal image (engraving) must be made of the art. This is achieved through a process called photoengraving. Essentially, photoengraving is a method of photographically re-creating line and/or continuous tone art on a metal printing plate. The following is a simplification of the complex method employed to make such plates. For our purpose, we will concentrate on understanding the *principle* and *essence* of this process rather than becoming involved too deeply in the mechanics.

LINE ART

First, a photographic film negative is made of the art. Then a sheet of polished zinc, copper, or magnesium metal, sensitized to light with a chemical solution and whirled to dry evenly, is placed under the negative in a vacuum frame and exposed to powerful lights. Those areas of the plate exposed to the light become acid resistant; i.e., in the photo negative the line appears clear, permitting the passage of light. The white areas of the original art are opaque on the photo negative, blocking out the light. The metal plate is then developed and is ready for etching.

The plate is given a bath in a solution of nitric acid, which eats away the

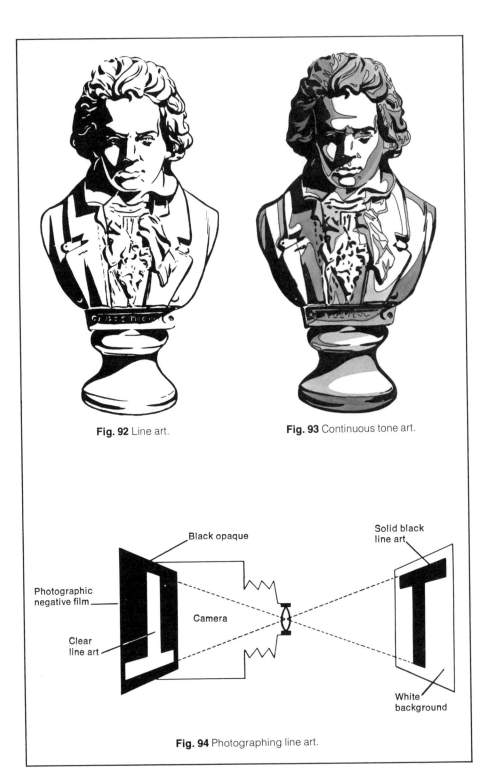

Fig. 92 Line art.

Fig. 93 Continuous tone art.

Black opaque

Solid black
line art

Photographic
negative film

Camera

Clear
line art

White
background

Fig. 94 Photographing line art.

unprotected metal to a shallow depth; it is then rinsed and dried. After a number of procedures and processings (which are unnecessary to go into for our purpose) the plate is completed and ready for printing. The result is a metal plate containing etched-out areas, leaving in raised portions an exact replica, in reverse position, of the original art. These raised portions, when covered with ink and pressed to paper, will leave an identical impression of the original art—similar to the common rubber stamp (Figs. 94, 95, 96, and 97).

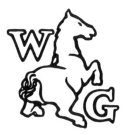

Fig. 95 Original line art.

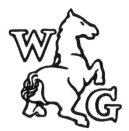

Fig. 96 Line art printed from a line plate.

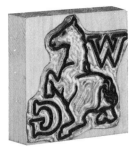

Fig. 97 Line plate (or cut) with the line in raised portions (relief).

CONTINUOUS TONE ART

A process similar to that used in the making of a line plate is followed with continuous tone art, except that a "screen" must be used in making the photographic negative. Printing is done with one color of ink, not different values of that color. In order to achieve the effect or illusion of continuous tone, the art must be converted to a "halftone" plate.

The halftone plate is made by inserting a ruled screen between the camera lens and the sensitized film. The screen is made up of diagonal crosshatched lines, varying from 55 to 155 lines per linear inch (a 55 screen, for example, contains 3,025 squares per square inch). Reflected light passing through the square screen openings break down the original art into various sized squares and dots on the negative. In white and light areas on the plate, the dots are smaller than in dark and black areas. That is, just as the value changes from white to black, so does the size of the dots change from small to large (Figs. 98, 99, and 100). Although the

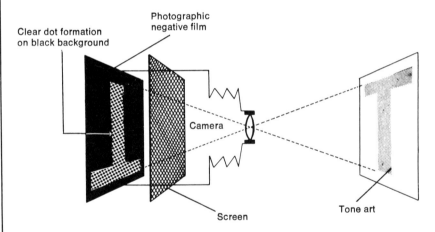

Fig. 98 Photographing continuous tone art.

Fig. 99 Here is a value change, from light to dark.

Fig. 100 Small dots in light areas get progressively larger until they merge into each other, creating the illusion of a white dot on black in the dark areas. (In the negative, the black dot is clear on a black background.)

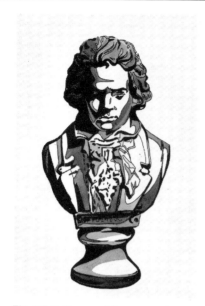

Fig. 101 To the eye, this appears to be continuous tone.

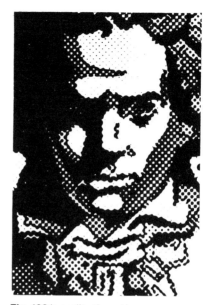

Fig. 102 In reality, the art is a composite of dots of various sizes.

images consist of dots and squares, they are generally referred to as "dots" or simply the "screen."

An example of halftone printing can be found in any daily newspaper. In viewing the picture at normal reading distance, note that the dot formation (screen) is not apparent. But upon closer examination (6" from the page or through a magnifying glass), you will be amazed to find that what appears to be a continuous blend of tones is really a maze of minute black dots of various sizes. Thus, printing with only *one color of ink*, this screen creates the phenomenal optical illusion of continuous tone (Figs. 101 and 102).

Because of the variety of processes of platemaking and printing, and the relevant terminology, I will refer to the individuals involved in the three stages of platemaking, regardless of process, as follows:

Cameraman: photographs the mechanical or art

Film stripper: handles the films and negatives for plating

Platemaker: does the actual plating

PHOTO RETOUCHING
With the exception of a few minor touches, the mechanical artist is not usually required to retouch photos. However, a good board artist should be able to do general retouching.

Because of the coarseness of newsprint paper, the dot (screen) must be

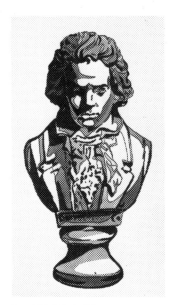

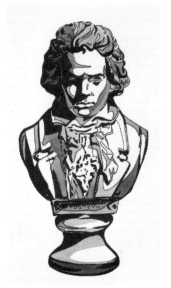

Fig. 103 This is 60 screen: you can see the dots.

Fig. 104 This is 85 screen: the dots are less obvious.

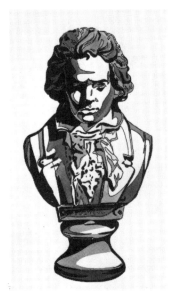

Fig. 105 This is 110 screen: the image is much sharper.

coarse. A fine screen will blur or fill in when printed, causing a poor reproduction. The photo or art work must, therefore, be coarse or retouched "hard," i.e., with a strong contrast of one value against the other. If the changes in value are blended or smooth, the coarse screen will lose much of the effect and detail, owing to the few large dots and spaces between the dots. However, if the changes are abrupt and of sharp tone contrast and have little detail, they will pick up in spite of the heavy dot. Newspapers, if printed by letterpress, generally use 50–65 screen; 85–110 screen is used in second-grade trade publications.

On the other hand, if the printing is being done on slick magazine stock, a finer screen (100–120 screen, depending on the slickness of the stock) may be used. However, most trade and consumer publications are printed by offset lithography, which uses a standard 133 (or finer) screen. Most newspapers are converting from letterpress to offset, using 85 screen or finer. The halftones in this book (for example) are printed in 133 screen. Under these conditions, the art or photo can be retouched with more detail and smooth blending of values. The dots in a finer screen, being smaller and more abundant, will pick up a better coverage of the areas, thus affording a truer reproduction. A 120–133 screen is used on enamel and other smooth-finished stocks, 150–175 on the highest coated only (Figs. 103, 104, and 105).

SQUARE HALFTONE
This is a plate (square or rectangular in shape) having right-angle corners, with its entire surface carrying a dot formation (Fig. 106).

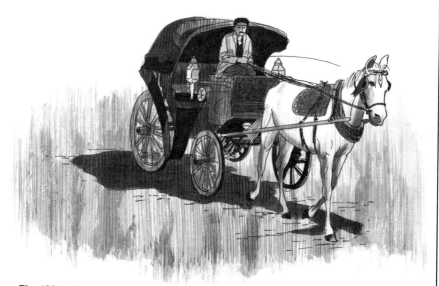

Fig. 106 In this image—a square halftone—there are no solid blacks or pure whites.

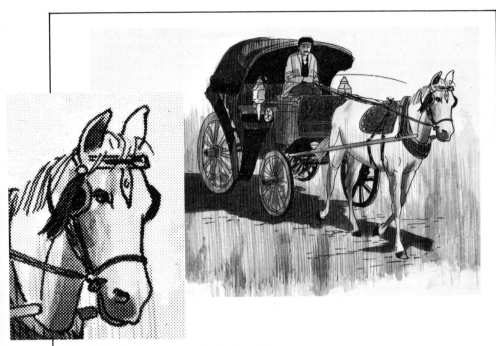

Fig. 107 Notice the dot formation in the white areas.

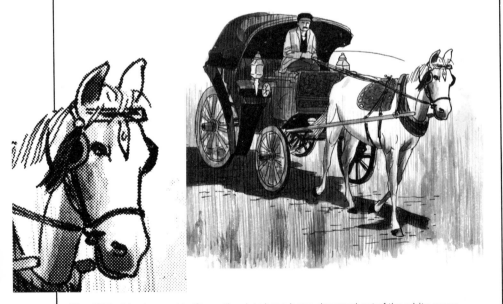

Fig. 108 In this drop-out halftone, the dots have been dropped out of the white areas.

DROP-OUT HALFTONE (HIGHLIGHT HALFTONE)

In a normal halftone of an illustration containing white areas, for example, pure white areas or highlights will appear white but actually contain a fine dot (see "Silhouette Halftone" below). In order to effect an actual white, these dots may be eliminated (dropped out) by the cameraman or film stripper (Figs. 107 and 108). This is much more effective in art work than in photos. Drop-out in photos should be done with discretion, or the result may look very false.

SILHOUETTE HALFTONE

If the original art is a shape on a white background and a square halftone plate is made, the white background would not be pure white. It would pick up a minute dot called "papertone." If a pure white background is desired, the shape will have to be silhouetted so that just the unit itself will contain the screen with an abrupt ending of dots at the silhouetted edge, then printed onto white paper. This is done by the cameraman or the film stripper, who will mask or opaque (on the negative) the screen surrounding any part of the image (Figs. 109, 110, and 111).

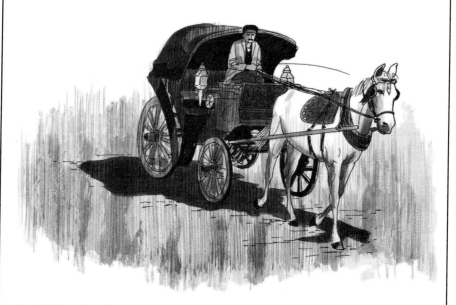

Fig. 109 Here the original art has been rendered on a white background.

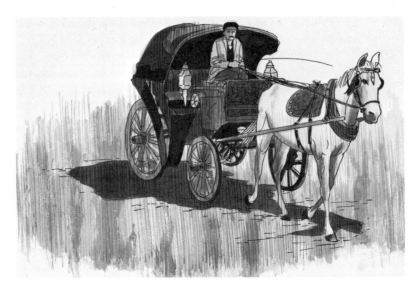

Fig. 110 Reproduced in square halftone, this art looks as if it had been done on a gray background.

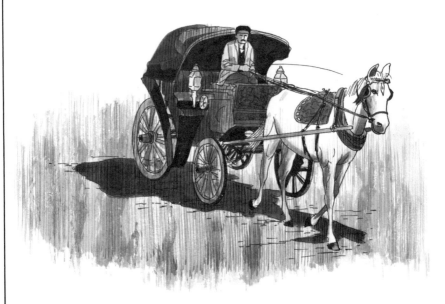

Fig. 111 By silhouetting the image, the dot formation on the background and within the art area has been eliminated.

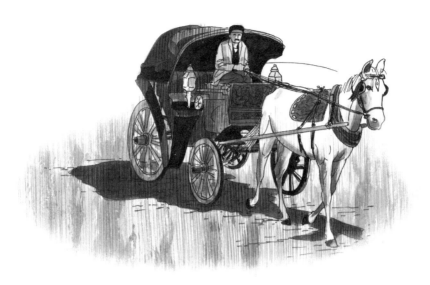

Fig. 112 The vignette halftone produces soft edges that blend into the paper.

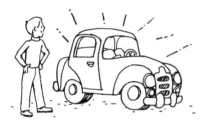

Fig. 113 A line illustration in black and white.

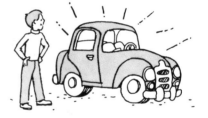

Fig. 114 With a screen, depth is added.

VIGNETTE HALFTONE

A vignette halftone is a halftone blending into the paper along the edges; i.e., the dots gradually decrease in size until they disappear at the edges of the art and blend into the surface of the paper (Fig. 112).

SCREENING

A screening is a mechanical application of dots, lines, or patterns used as a means of obtaining even values of black or color in conjunction with the line art (Figs. 113 and 114).

SURPRINT

In instances when line and halftone must appear as one unit, one superimposed over the other, but the line and continuous tone originals are separate pieces of art, a *surprint* is employed. For example, the layout calls for tone art with a line of black type across it (Fig. 115). By combining the two negatives (line and halftone), the platemaker will produce one plate of this arrangement, thus producing this effect in one printing.

Surprint must be a combination of line and halftone or screen (tint) of the *same color*, i.e., black on gray, solid red on a screen of red, solid green on a screen of green, etc. Solid red type on a gray photo or black type on a colored background are not examples of surprinting because two separate color plates and printings are required. If the line of type were white, instead of black, it would be considered a drop-out.

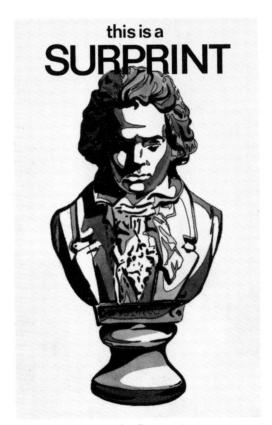

Fig. 115 This is a surprint: line over tone.

COMBINATION PLATE
When continuous tone and line art are to appear together, but as separate elements, separate negatives are made (halftone and line) and are combined into one plate (Fig. 116).

VELOX
If the cost of a halftone plate is too high to conform to the allocated budget, a method by which halftone effects may be achieved at a lower cost is employed. The original art is photographically converted to a halftone negative and printed onto a photographic paper in positive form called Velox. Because the Velox can be made to the required reproduction size and is composed of "line" dots, it may be placed in position on the mechanical to be used as finished art. The mechanical can then be shot completely in line.

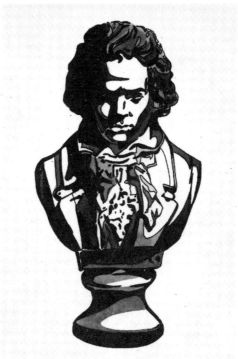

this is a
COMBINATION

Fig. 116 A combination plate is made by combining tone and line art on one plate.

Usually, the combined cost of Velox and line plates is less than the cost of a complete plate (line and halftone) made by the platemaker. This is especially true when silhouette and drop-out Veloxes are used.

In addition to the advantage of converting the continuous tone into halftone, the dots of the Velox can be retouched by the artist with white or black paint, or dropped out, or made into a combination of line and halftone by the Velox cameraman; thus, the artist has more control over the desired effects. Surprint Veloxes are obtainable, and Velox prints also come in nearly the same variety of screens as do metal plates. Line prints of type or drawings can be made instead of stats for better-quality reproduction.

The term *Velox* in itself does not mean halftone. It is the name of the type of paper used. This paper can be used to make ordinary line prints as well as halftones. Therefore, the true terminology should be "Line" Velox and "Halftone" Velox, but this seems to create confusion. So a "Line" Velox is referred to simply as a line print.

When using Veloxes for newspaper reproduction, you will notice that the reproduction proof has a tendency to be darker. In order to compensate for this fill-in, the Velox should have a flat look, not be as contrasty as you would expect it to appear in the paper. In such a case, instruct the Velox house to hold an "open dot."

DUPLICATING ADVERTISEMENTS

Frequently, the client will want to run the same ad in more than one newspaper at the same time. The various printing processes have different mechanical requirements in conjunction with preferred printing materials. In order to accommodate these requirements, printing seldom is done directly from the original metal engraving. Duplicates of an entire advertisement (including the type) are needed in order to run an advertisement in several different periodicals simultaneously if the printing process is letterpress. Many duplicate copies can be reproduced at a fraction of the cost of the original. One such substitute (to save time and expense) is the electrotype ("electro") made from the original engraving and used as the printing plate. Duplicate *molds* (called stereotype mats or matrices) can be made from this electro or directly from the original engraving.

These molds, made of a type of composition papier-mâché, are reasonably light and durable. They can be mailed or shipped to any part of the country, and duplicates of the original engraving can be made from them at a relatively low cost. The duplicates are made by pouring a molten lead composition into the mold. In addition to the paper mat, a plastic mat also can be made which may better serve the same purpose. Plastic plates are beginning to supplement the electrotype.

COLOR SEPARATION

Under present commercial printing conditions only one color, with one plate, can be printed onto paper at a time. Therefore, in order to re-create, by printing, a color photo or art work, *separate* printing plates must be prepared for *each color*.

This is achieved during the process of plate preparation by use of an intricate photographic filtration system. The result is a separate plate for each color to be printed. Each plate represents the correct proportion of each color necessary to create the full color of the original. Actually, only four colors are required to create a full-color effect: magenta, cyan, yellow, and black. In printing, black is considered a color. This method of printing is called *process color* printing. However, art that is to be printed in two or three colors (other than process color) must be mechanically prepared. That is to say that the printing plates are not prepared by the filtration process. The art, to begin with, does not exist in color. It must be mechanically created by the artist and cameraman. The procedure employed in its preparation is called *mechanical color separation*.

In essence, this kind of reproduction is achieved through a combination of effort between the artist, the film stripper, and the platemaker. The artist must clearly instruct and/or provide the film stripper with the proper description and/or material to achieve the desired end result.

Basically, the artist uses two methods. One is "indicating" to the film stripper what and where the color is to appear. The film stripper will then prepare the film according to the artist's indications and instructions. This is done by using a method called *keyline* indication. The other method is to provide the film stripper with the actual shape of the color positioned in the proper place on the art or mechanical. This is called the *overlay* method.

Study Fig. 117. The desired effect is black type printed over a color or surprinting a tint of black or tint of color. Now let's consider the methods used to achieve it.

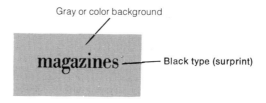

Gray or color background

magazines —— Black type (surprint)

Fig. 117 This is the effect that is desired: black type over a gray or color background.

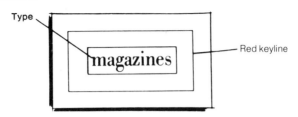

Fig. 118 In the keyline method, the desired area is outlined with a thin red or black line directly in position on the mechanical, the type cemented in position.

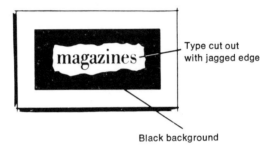

Fig. 119 In the solid black fill-in method of indicating color separation, the area is filled in with solid black directly in position on the mechanical, and the line of type is cut out with a jagged edge and cemented into position.

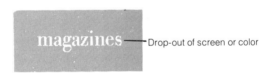

Fig. 120 This is the desired effect: type dropped out of screen.

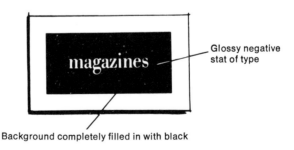

Fig. 121 Use a glossy negative stat to indicate position.

KEYLINE

In this method of indicating color separation, the desired area is outlined with a thin red or black line directly in position on the art or mechanical with the line of type cemented in position. This thin red or black line acts as a guide for the film stripper (Fig. 118). It indicates a description of the exact size, shape, and position of the color element.

The outline itself is not retained in plating unless such is so indicated. Black and red will photograph the same; however, of the two colors, red is more widely used. The reason obviously is the fact that if a screen tint area is outlined in red, there is no question about whether or not the outline should be retained in plating; i.e., the reproduction will appear as a gray area with no outline.

On the other hand, if the area were outlined in black and no indication were made to delete this line on the negative, the area would appear when printed as gray (screen) with a black outline. If black outlines are to be used for such indications, they should be neatly "X'd" out with blue pencil or ink with instructions in the margin to indicate their deletion.

SOLID BLACK FILL-IN

In this variation of indicating color separation, the area is filled in with solid black directly in position on the mechanical, and the line of type is cut out with a jagged edge and cemented in position (Fig. 119). In cutting the jagged edges, do not cut too close to the live matter. On the other hand, if the layout indicates a reverse or drop-out type in that area (Fig. 120), a glossy negative stat of the type may be cemented into proper position (Fig. 121).

However, *only when stats are not available* for one reason or another may you prepare it as in Figs. 118 or 119 and indicate instructions for the line to be dropped out of the screen. The positive may also be cemented onto a sheet of acetate or vellum taped over the mechanical (see "Overlay," page 78).

When type or art is to surprint or drop out of a *halftone* instead of a screen tint, the same procedure is followed, i.e., using a matte stat of the tone art as a guide for size and position in the mechanical and cementing the line of type (cut out with a jagged edge) onto the stat in position or on an acetate overlay.

In shapes or areas of screen tint that may butt against a solid or another screen tint, a jagged edge of those shapes separating one from the other is used to retain the proper outline (Figs. 122 and 123). Butting one screen tint against the other should be done with discretion and the realization that the joining edges may create a moiré pattern or an irregular black line as a result of improper aligning of the rows of the screen dots.

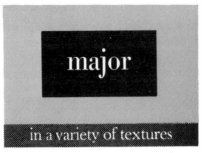

Fig. 122 In this instance, two screen values are being used.

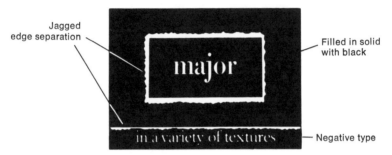

Jagged edge separation

Filled in solid with black

major

Negative type

Fig. 123 To prepare the mechanical for Fig. 122, butt one screen against another.

OVERLAY

In this method of preparing color separation, the shape may be outlined in light blue ink or pencil directly in position on the mechanical and the line of type cemented in position (Fig. 124). Light blue will not register on the cameraman's negative; it is used as a visual guide. Then a sheet of vellum or acetate, taped across the top, is placed over the mechanical. Registration marks must be drawn on the original mechanical in black ink outside the mechanical (live) area and corresponding marks accurately traced in ink on the overlay of vellum or acetate.

The outlined shape is then *completely* inked in with solid black on the overlay with no jagged edge (Fig. 125). If the line of type were to be dropped out of the background (as in Fig. 120), there would be no need for the overlay. This overlay acts as an individual mechanical for the color or screen tint area and automatically separates it from the type, which obviates a good deal of work for the film stripper.

The corresponding blue outline is not always used in conjunction with the overlay; it is merely a precaution—a sort of belt and suspenders arrangement. Sometimes a red line is used for the same purpose.

A red color film sheet may be used in place of black ink on the overlay; the unwanted portions (outside the blue line) are scratched or cut away.

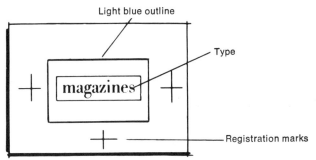

Light blue outline

Type

magazines

Registration marks

Fig. 124 In the overlay method of color separating, registration marks are a must.

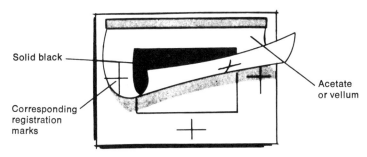

Solid black

Acetate
or vellum

Corresponding
registration
marks

Fig. 125 Ink the outlined shape completely with solid black on the overlay.

Deep, warm red or dark orange films can be used for overlays because they photograph the same as black. Because they are translucent, they afford better visualization of the areas as they will appear in relation to one another. Each overlay *must* have registration marks to correspond with the art beneath it to ensure perfect alignment of all elements.

Cover the art or mechanical with clear acetate. Then, using an adhesive-backed color film, cut and peel away a section large enough to cover the area to be done. Lightly burnish it onto the clear acetate over the specific area. Cut around the areas and shapes (Fig. 126) and peel away the unwanted portions (Fig. 127). Then burnish in place. Use a clean razor blade or X-acto knife; a light pressure is all that is required to cut this film. After the excess is removed, there will be a residue of wax left on the acetate. It can be rubbed off with a clean, dry handkerchief. Do not use cotton for this.

A material that performs the same function but comes in another color is the ruby- or amber-colored film. This medium has a rubberlike coating on polyester film that can be cut and peeled away, exposing the clear film. It is convenient because of the ease and cleanliness with which it can be handled. Both the ruby and amber photograph as black.

If you accidentally scratch or cut away a needed portion of the film

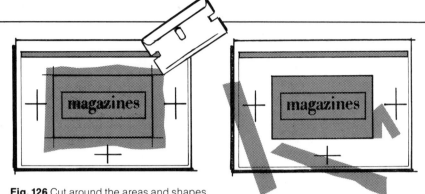

Fig. 126 Cut around the areas and shapes. Do not cut through the acetate.

Fig. 127 Peel away unwanted portions.

when working with color films or ruby- and amber-colored film, you can touch it up with black acetate ink. It may not look very neat, but these colors and black photograph the same. Actually, you can use a combination of adhesive color film or ruby-colored film in conjunction with inking in of detail in black on the overlay; i.e., a job consisting of large masses as well as detail shapes can be done with this medium by using the ruby-colored film as the entire overlay. Then cut and peel away the unwanted areas, including the entire portion that takes in the detail. Ink in the detail on the exposed acetate. Deep red (water-base) photo opaquing paint is excellent for this purpose.

SELF-APPLIED SCREENING OR SHADING SHEETS
Among other widely used materials for achieving tints of color effects are textured commercial "shading" sheets. The adhesive-backed film of desired texture or tint is placed in position on the mechanical or art and carefully cut out. The undesired areas are taken off, and the remaining portion is burnished in position (Figs. 128, 129, and 130). This eliminates much work for the film stripper, cuts down on the cost of the plate, and enables the artist to control the effects accordingly. Instructions for its use are clearly indicated on the sheet. An example of this method can be found in the cartoon section of any daily newspaper.

When you are working with self-applied shading sheets, little bubbles often appear on the surface as a result of air being trapped beneath. This will interfere with reproduction. Puncture the bubbles lightly with a fine needle or push pin, then burnish gently to force the air out.

The surface of most shading sheets will accept ink in the event you have to do additional work in an area after it has been burnished into position. Try an acetate ink. The ink can conveniently be wiped off with wet tissue.

Bear in mind that the method of reproduction will determine the screen *size* you may use. Each size screen pattern comes in a variety of gray values (10%, 20%, 30%, etc.). Be certain that you do not confuse the

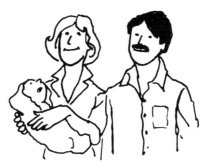

Fig. 128 The original line art.

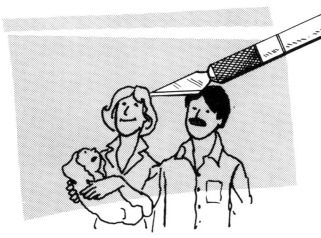

Fig. 129 Place the film over the art and cut.

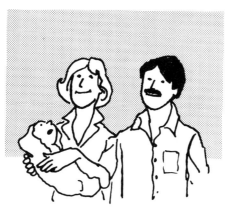

Fig. 130 Peel away unwanted pieces and burnish the sheet into position.

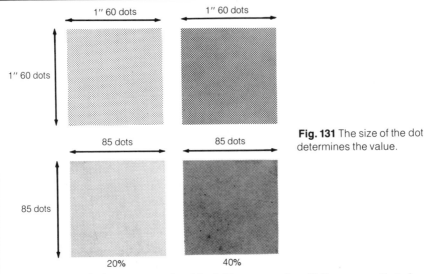

1" 60 dots   1" 60 dots

1" 60 dots

85 dots   85 dots

Fig. 131 The size of the dot determines the value.

85 dots

20%   40%

screen *size* with the screen *value* (tint). For example, all the screen tints in a 60 screen have the *same number of dots*. The value change is the result of the dots being larger or smaller; i.e., the dots in a 20% tint are smaller than those in a 40% tint. An 85 screen, 40% tint has the same number of dots as an 85 screen, 20% tint; only the size of the dot changes, not the quantity (Fig. 131).

EXAMPLES OF APPLICATION

Fig. 132 represents a layout consisting of black type surprinting on a screen tint of black or color background and white type on a black background. Using the methods described above, the mechanical for this layout may be prepared in the ways shown in Figs. 133, 134, and 135.

At the completion of any such mechanical, a color guide (breakdown) must be made for the printer and platemaker. This is done by placing a tissue over the entire mechanical (taped across the top) and filling in the desired color shapes. On a black and white job, screen areas are indicated in gray. Colored pencils or markers are usually used for this purpose.

Regardless of the method used, the result from each mechanical will be identical. The method used depends upon the nature of the desired effect, the means of reproduction, and the costs involved.

Any combination of the same methods might be employed. The more colors involved, the more variations of separation can be worked out. For example, in a three-color mechanical (black, green, and red) you might use any one of the approaches illustrated in Figs. 137 to 141 to obtain the required results. Fig. 136 represents the layout. Note that in all cases the *black* areas are always filled in solid. The *color of the keyline* has no bearing on the *color to be printed*. (For further information on this subject see *Mechanical Color Separation Skills* by the author.)

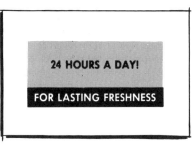

Fig. 132 Here is the desired effect: black type surprinting on a screen tint of black or color background and white type on a black background. This background can be a screen of black (gray), solid color, or a screen of color.

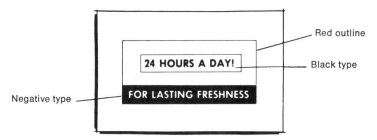

Fig. 133 The keyline method.

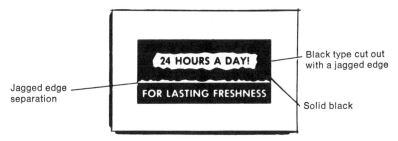

Fig. 134 The solid black fill-in method.

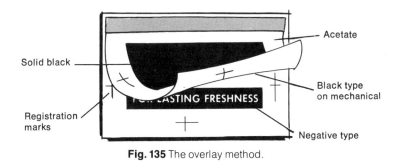

Fig. 135 The overlay method.

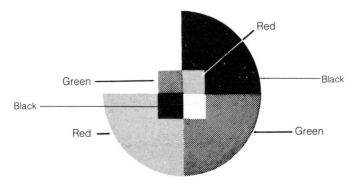

Fig. 136 The desired effect: three colors.

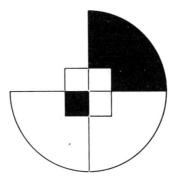

Fig. 137 The keyline method. Color areas are outlined in red. Black is filled in solid black.

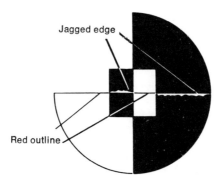

Fig. 138 Here is a combination of a solid black fill-in for one color and a keyline for the other color. Note: the jagged edge should appear only on one side. The edge of the completely filled-in side also acts as the edge of the color to butt against it.

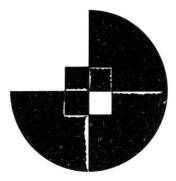

Fig. 139 Here both colors are filled in solid black. Note the jagged edges.

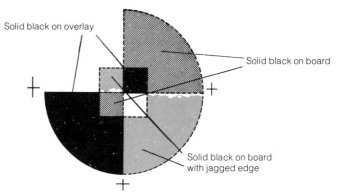

Fig. 140 Here the indication is made with one overlay and solid black fill-in. The black and green areas are filled in with solid black on the mechanical. The red areas are filled in with black on an acetate overlay.

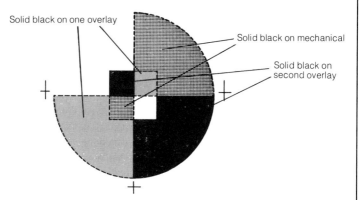

Fig. 141 This method employs two overlays. No jagged edge separation is needed. The black areas are filled in on the mechanical; the red areas are filled in with black on one overlay; the green areas are filled in with black on the second overlay.

CHAPTER 5

PRINTING PROCESSES

T HE FOLLOWING are the basic printing processes from which many methods of printing emanate. The purpose of this book is not to elaborate on production methods but simply to act as a vehicle of familiarization. These principles will supply you with the basics for understanding how the printed page is made.

LETTERPRESS (RELIEF PRINTING)
The printing surface (engraving), being raised, is covered with ink and pressed against the paper, thus transferring the image. Forms of relief printing surfaces include electrotypes, photoengravings, and type (Fig. 142). Until a few years ago, the majority of daily newspapers were printed in this method. However, offset lithography is currently the major commercial printing method.

GRAVURE (INTAGLIO)
The printing surface of the intaglio plate is the reverse of letterpress: its image is in the form of a depression rather than raised. The plate is covered with ink and wiped off, leaving ink deposits only in the depressions (or cells) of various depths. When the plate is pressed against the paper, the ink is sucked from these cells, leaving the image upon the surface of the paper. Examples of intaglio printing are photogravure and rotogravure (Fig. 143), which can be found in weekly supplements.

OFFSET (PLANOGRAPHIC PRINTING)
The surface of the plate in offset lithography is neither intaglio nor relief, but flat or planographic. The fact that water and grease do not

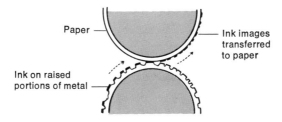

Fig. 142 This is the basis of letterpress printing.

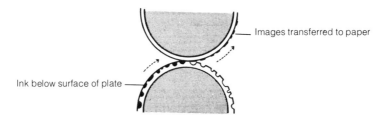

Fig. 143 This is the basis for intaglio (gravure) printing.

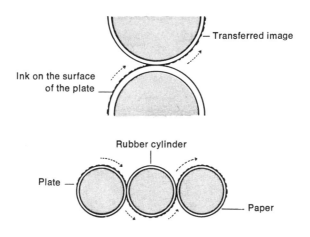

Fig. 144 This is the basis for offset printing.

mix is the principle of offset printing. The areas of the plate which are not to be printed are treated to give them an affinity to water. Before each printing, water is applied to the surface of the plate. The water repels the ink, which is greasy; the untreated areas retain the ink. In offset printing the plate does not transfer the image directly to the paper but to a rubber cylinder (mat) and then to the paper (Fig. 144).

In letterpress printing the type and/or "cuts" (engravings) are separate pieces and must be assembled for printing. This makes it possible to effect changes simply by replacing the particular cut or type (Fig. 145). In offset, the photographic negatives of type and art are assembled, and one complete printing plate is made from the negatives. Because each element is in its proper position as a single unit, it is impossible to effect a major change in the plate once it has been made. The same is true of intaglio printing (Fig. 146). Nevertheless, offset lithography is the fastest and probably the least expensive of all methods.

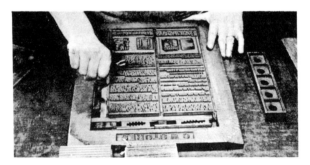

Fig. 145 This is a letterpress form, composed of separate pieces of metal.

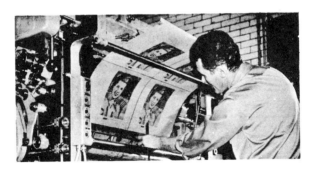

Fig. 146 Unlike the letterpress plate, the offset plate is a sheet of flexible metal.

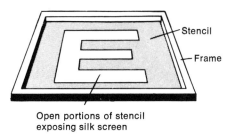

Stencil

Frame

Open portions of stencil
exposing silk screen

Fig. 147 In silk screen printing, a stencil is affixed to a screen.

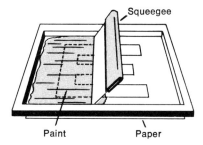

Squeegee

Paint   Paper

Fig. 148 A squeegee forces the ink through the openings in the stencil and screen.

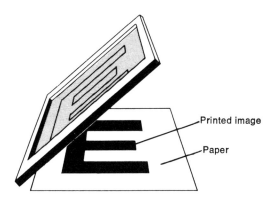

Printed image

Paper

Fig. 149 The end result of a silk screen print.

SILK SCREEN PRINTING

Silk screen is a process of printing through a stencil that is permanently affixed to a screen of silk (Fig. 147).

The open areas of the stencil permit paint to be forced through the exposed underlying screen mesh, while penetration of paint through the masked or blocked-out areas is impossible (Figs. 148 and 149).

The masked area, as a whole, may be prepared by using tusche, paper, old-fashioned block-outs, hand-cut film, or photographic film.

The screen mesh itself is made of a fine weave of silk, which permits an even flow and coverage of paint in printing. Silk is used because of its strength and durability.

In order to meet the demands of commercial requirements, intricate power-operated presses are used. Both the flat and rotary presses are excellent for printing continuous patterns on almost any material in both line and halftone. The most practical applications of silk screen are utilized in the textile industry and for printing on unusual surfaces such as wood, glass, leather, etc.

Some of the advantages of this process are the achievement of brilliant color effects, the ability to print on difficult surfaces, the exclusion of expensive color plates, the ability to print on surfaces too large for standard printing presses, and the low cost in producing limited quantities.

CHAPTER 6

FOLDING AND TRIMMING

I<small>N</small> <small>PREPARING</small> mechanicals for pieces such as those described in this chapter, trim size and fold areas must be indicated. A *dash* line means fold; a *solid* line means trim (crop marks). These lines must be indicated in red or black ink on the mechanical outside of the trim edge and should not extend into the bleed area (Fig. 150). A thin blue line is often drawn around the trim edge as a visual aid.

BLEED

Bleed is employed in magazines, brochures, mailing pieces, posters, or any such printed piece that must be cut to a specific size or shape (die cut). When such a piece is designed to have "live matter" (art, color, tone, etc.) run off the edge, allowances must be made for the cutting process. For example, the dummy specifies that a band of color is to run along and off the bottom edge and both sides of a mailing piece (Fig. 151).

In making the mechanical you must indicate not just the actual coverage of the color, but an additional ⅛"—no less—from the trim edge wherever the color runs off the page (Fig. 152). This will provide extra color area in the event that the cutting should be somewhat inaccurate. If just the actual coverage were printed (stopping at the trim edge) and the cutting were off slightly, a white edge would appear, resulting in a poor effect. Therefore, this extra coverage or bleed is used as a precaution (Fig. 153).

By the same token, if the layout calls for live matter to run very close to the edge, but not off (such as a line of type), be certain that you do not place it closer than permitted, according to the requirements of the printer. Should the type be too close to the edge and the cutting be off, the type also may be cut into.

Study the folds shown in Fig. 154.

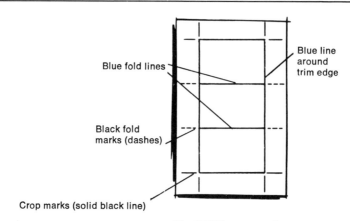

Blue fold lines

Blue line around trim edge

Black fold marks (dashes)

Crop marks (solid black line)

Fig. 150 When preparing mechanicals, note the difference between fold marks and trim marks.

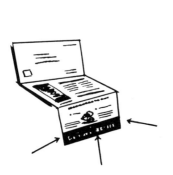

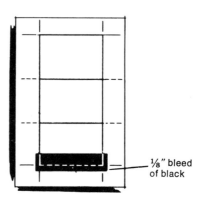

⅛" bleed of black

Fig. 151 The band of color runs off the edge of this piece: it is a bleed.

Fig. 152 To indicate a bleed on the mechanical, carry the color an additional ⅛" beyond the trim mark.

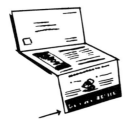

Fig. 153 If you neglect to carry the color beyond the trim mark, you may find an undesirable white edge appearing in the final piece.

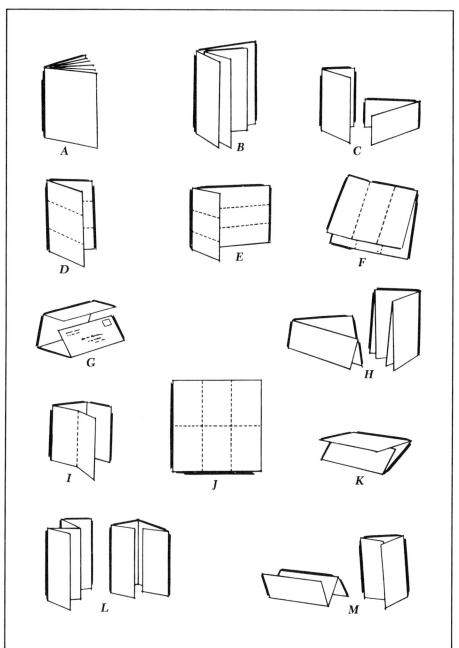

Fig. 154 Study these folds. (**A**) ordinary booklet; (**B**) eight-page booklet; (**C**) four-page folder; (**D**) four-page letter; (**E**) six-page folder with short fold; (**F**) broadside with one short fold; (**G**) single-fold or two-fold card mailing piece; (**H**) French-fold; (**I**) eight-page folder with short fold; (**J**) regular broadside; (**K**) two-fold mailing piece; (**L**) eight-page folder with two folds; (**M**) six-page folder.

CHAPTER 7

TRICKS OF
THE TRADE

Now that the basics of the process of producing mechanicals have been described, here are some tricks of the trade which should be of use to you in particular assignments you may receive.

HOW TO USE A RULING PEN
In spite of his or her manual dexterity, the surgeon cannot perform efficiently with an inferior instrument. So it is with artists and their tools. It has been said that a good artist can do a good job in spite of the condition of the equipment used. This does *not* apply to the use of the ruling pen. The most skilled craftsman will have difficulty executing quality work with a pen that is not in good condition. Likewise, a good tool in the hands of the incompetent will result in both inferior work and possible damage to the tool.

A good ruling pen is a prerequisite to making efficient mechanicals. The most convenient type is the jackknife, or any such type that allows for proper cleaning. The less expensive pens are not of much use; they wear out quickly or do not rule clean lines. Your ruling pen should be kept clean while not in use. Never allow the ink to dry or form a crust around the point. If this should happen, clean it with ammonia or with water. Never scrape off dried ink or paint with a razor blade. Cleaning the pen frequently with water and a rag while it is in use will avoid stoppage of ink flow and broken lines.

These simple rules will ensure professional and accurate results:

Fill the pen by using a dropper, placing it about ½" up from the point. Be careful not to overload the pen. *Never dip your pen into the ink*. Be certain that the outside of the blades is clean before performing, or blotches and poor lines will result (Fig. 155).

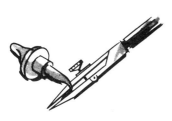

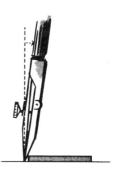

Fig. 155 Loading the ruling pen.

Fig. 156 Create a triangular space between the tip of the pen and the straightedge. Tilt the pen slightly back.

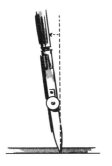

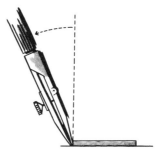

Fig. 157 Tilt the pen slightly to the side.

Fig. 158 If you tilt the pen forward, the ink will pull under the straightedge and blotch.

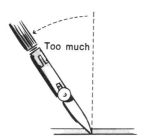

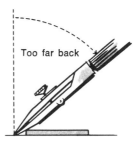

Fig. 159 If you tilt the pen too much to the side, you will get poor contact with the surface, resulting in inaccurate lines.

Fig. 160 Do not tilt the pen back too much. Not only will the contact be poor—consequently producing a poor line—but you will also damage the pen.

Hold the pen with thumb and index finger in alignment with the second digit of the index finger—the screw adjustment facing out. Line up your straightedge directly on the pencil line. Now pull the straightedge away from the pencil line (about $\frac{1}{32}''$).

Position the pen along the straightedge at a right angle to the surface, resting the last three fingers on the surface of the straightedge. Tilt it back and to the right *very slightly* so that the tip of the pen touches the pencil line. This will enable you to see the point without leaning over and also to create a triangular space between the tip of the pen and the straightedge (Figs. 156 and 157).

Slide the pen in this position along the edge without bending your wrist or elbow. *Do not press* the pen. The action should take place in the movement of your shoulders and arm as a unit. Never *push* your ruling pen. Whenever possible, the line to be drawn should be parallel to the shoulder line, even if it means turning the board or body. To obtain proper results, keep in mind that the direction of the stroke should be from left to right, or *away* from the body.

Do not tilt the pen forward. This will cause the ink to pull under the straightedge and blotch (Fig. 158). *Do not tilt* it back or to the side too far. Poor and inaccurate lines will result, in addition to wearing the points unevenly, subsequently destroying the efficiency of the pen (Figs. 159 and 160).

To prevent blotches and smears resulting from the pen in contact with the straightedge, some artists tape two pennies, or some other device, such as a triangle, blotter, etc., beneath the straightedge to lift the edge from the board. This is effective, but it may scratch or damage the elements in the mechanical. Use with discretion. In order to get the feel of the ruling pen, it would help to experiment with the above rules. Practice drawing lines of various thicknesses and lengths in order that you may learn the limitations of your pen (Fig. 161).

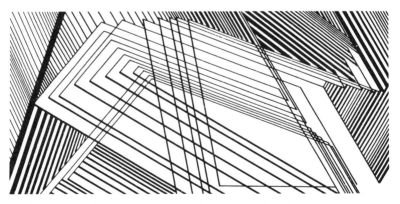

Fig. 161 Practice drawing lines of varying widths and lengths.

Vertical lines should be ruled along the *left* side of a triangle. For one thing, the direction of light is from the left, permitting better vision of the line. More important is the fact that the line should be drawn parallel to the shoulder line (or reasonably so). Therefore, if you turn your body until your shoulders are parallel to the line, you will find that drawing the line on the left side of the triangle and away from the body can be done more efficiently and with greater freedom.

However, if drawn along the right edge, the stroke would be toward the body, causing a cramped position; and, too, there is a tendency to tip the pen forward in an attempt to see the line (which is in shadow). This causes blotting. Should it be *necessary* to draw a vertical line at the extreme right of the T-square, and drawing the vertical line along the *right edge* of the triangle is *unavoidable*, stand, lean over the board, and twist your left shoulder toward the line (your right shoulder away); then draw from *left to right*.

TECHNICAL PENS

There are a number of ink-reservoir pens available that are unquestionably handy and much simpler to use than the ruling pen. However, the student should learn to use the ruling pen effectively rather than to rely completely upon the technical pen. While it may be difficult to use at first, there are many problems that a ruling pen can solve much more effectively: it is several pens in one, inasmuch as you can control and change the weight of line in an instant, can draw on surfaces the technical pen cannot draw on, and can be used for various colors of line without difficulty. Water paint or poster paint can be diluted enough to be used in the pen, which is very helpful when changes or revision of color line is necessary. Needless to say, a ruling pen line is probably the cleanest line possible.

Admittedly, though, this pen is difficult, if not often impossible, to use with certain templates such as small ellipses, circles, etc. For these purposes, the technical pen is, of course, your best tool. It should always be kept clean and in working order. Purchase a jar of pen cleaner, or use ammonia to keep the nibs clean. If your budget permits, you can have one for red, blue, and black ink. The technical pen is very useful in mechanical work. For the most part the same rules apply to use of the technical pen as for the ruling pen.

USE OF BRUSH AND RULER

You will often have occasion to draw clean, straight lines on a painted surface, photograph, or surface that would cause a blurry or broken line if the ruling pen were used. A particularly useful method of producing clean lines under such conditions is to use the brush with the ruler (referred to as a "bridge").

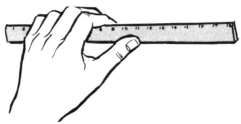

Fig. 162 Holding the ruler in this way, drop the heel of the hand to the board without touching the surface with your fingers.

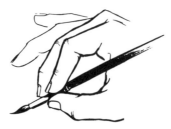

Fig. 163 Hold the brush between the thumb and middle finger of the right hand, resting the index finger high on the ferrule.

Fig. 164 Place the remaining fingers behind the ferrule and against the thumb.

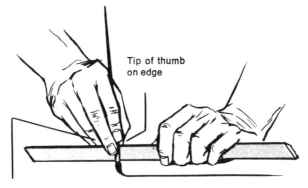

Tip of thumb
on edge

Fig. 165 Place the ferrule against the metal edge of the ruler so that the tip of the thumb rests upon this edge and the nail of the third finger lies flat against the front of the ruler.

For a straightedge, a *thick* metal-edged wooden ruler is preferable; a thin wooden or metal ruler is too flexible. With the left hand, hold the ruler metal edge up, and place it in position on the surface to be ruled on so that the thumb rests half on the bottom edge of the ruler, half on the surface, while the fingers overlap and the fingernails rest flat against the surface on the opposite side, permitting a firm grip. Drop the heel of the hand to the surface (Fig. 162).

Hold the brush between the thumb and middle finger of the right hand, resting the index finger high on the ferrule (Fig. 163). Place the remaining fingers behind the ferrule and against the thumb (Fig. 164). Position the ferrule of the brush against the metal edge of the ruler so that the tip of the thumb rests upon this edge and the nail of the third finger lies flat against the front of the ruler (Fig. 165).

While some artists prefer to rest the nail of the middle finger against the ruler, I feel that the position just described affords a firmer grip. Some artists turn the hand slightly and rest just the tip of the thumb on the edge or side of the ruler, thus pressing the ferrule against the edge between the thumb and index finger.

Now, bring the brush into contact with the paper by pushing forward with the index and middle fingers. Move it along the edge, keeping an even pressure throughout. Keep the wrist high—do not twist it. To achieve a firm line, avoid too slow an action; develop a smooth, brisk stroke.

To vary the thickness of the line, simply vary the pressure of the fingers on the brush. The paint should be of a consistency just thin enough to flow freely from the brush.

Another advantage of this method is in silhouetting straight lines on photos when a pen might scratch the surface or deposit too heavy a layer of paint.

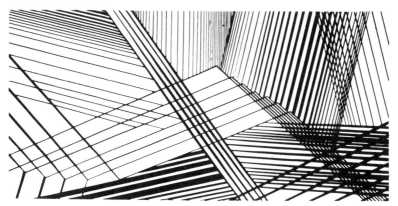

Fig. 166 Practice using the brush and ruler with lines of varying lengths and widths.

INKING

Clean corners are a *must* in inking. Whenever possible, draw the connecting line with the straightedge away from the adjoining line (Figs. 167 and 168). This will lessen the danger of pulling the ink under the straightedge, which would result in blotting.

Where heavy lines are needed (beyond the capacity of the pen in one stroke), it is best, especially if you are using the ruling pen, to build them up rather than to attempt them in one stroke (Fig. 169).

Sometimes a line is drawn too short and must be made longer. In that case, at the beginning of the connecting stroke, position the point above the paper and slightly to the left of the intersection. Then, with a sweeping motion, bring the pen into contact with the paper, blending one line into the other.

In drawing wide lines, it is sometimes best to ink in the outer edges and

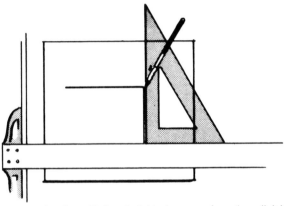

Fig. 167 Draw the connecting line with the straightedge away from the adjoining line.

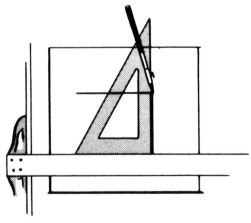

Fig. 168 Do not place the triangle over the connecting line as shown here.

fill them in with a pen or brush. Do not make the outline too thin, or it may be difficult to paint up to it without going beyond (Figs. 170 and 171).

To make corners with heavy or wide lines, draw a *thin* line to the point of the corner and build it up a little with a few more strokes; these additional strokes should *not* be drawn all the way. Then fill in with a brush or pen. This will prevent heavy blobs of ink deposits at the corners, thus avoiding blotching or round corners (Fig. 172).

Do not be afraid to use white paint to point up corners or lines. But do it *neatly*. Thick, sloppy patches of white paint do not necessarily interfere with the reproduction, but they give a very messy and unprofessional appearance. Some artists prefer to crisscross their corners and later sharpen them up with white paint (Fig. 173). This is a poor habit to develop because it is a waste of time. It is just as easy to learn to ink up to the point of the corner.

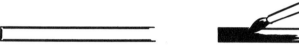

Fig. 169 If you want a thick line, build it up with a succession of thin strokes with the pen.

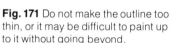

Fig. 170 In drawing wide lines, it is sometimes best to ink in the outer edges and fill them in with a pen or brush.

Fig. 171 Do not make the outline too thin, or it may be difficult to paint up to it without going beyond.

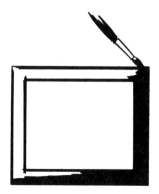

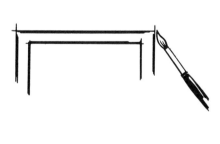

Fig. 172 Fill in the lines with a brush or pen.

Fig. 173 Corners can be crisscrossed, then touched up later with white paint.

In the event that an inking job is smeared beyond repair, simply redo it on a separate piece of paper (Strathmore), cut it out neatly, and cement it over the damaged area.

Should a line drawing of this nature have to be cut out, do not cut too close to the live edge unless it is unavoidable. Cutting too close to the edge may damage the line or cast a shadow during filming, resulting in a poor reproduction. All paste-up and cut marks will pick up on the negative and must be deleted by the film stripper before plating; if they are too close to the edge of the art, it is difficult for the opaquer to delete them.

DASH LINES

Measuring the dash and space precisely with a ruler is a tedious and often unnecessary time waster. Unless it is required, do not use this method.

Where just an effect is called for, you will save time and the results will be just as pleasing if you practice this simple approach.

Draw a continuous line; then, with white paint and brush, paint out the spaces by eye (Fig. 174). It may help to draw a dash at the beginning and one at the end of the line before starting. This helps to create a better illusion of evenness.

Your first attempt may not produce particularly good results. However, after a relatively short period of practice, your judgment will develop and surprising effects will begin to show.

Try this a few times: Draw a line about 3" long. Decide upon the length of the dash and the space. Then proceed as described above. The last stroke of white should leave the last dash the correct length. Try several until you get the feel of it (Fig. 175). Now, draw two lines forming a right-angle corner—and repeat (Fig. 176).

FREEHAND DASH

You may try drawing each dash with the pen rather than with the method just described. However, note that it is more difficult to control the overall effect and that the dash is not as clean when drawn this way (Fig. 177). You can, of course, use the adhesive-backed film (or tape) dash lines. Check the quality of this material; it is often poor.

ROUNDED CORNERS

Inking rounded corners can be troublesome if it is not approached in the proper manner. To begin with, unless the union of the straight line with the curve is exact, it will not look correct and will be difficult to rectify.

Using a 45° triangle, draw a diagonal line through A (see Fig. 178). If a 45° triangle is not available, pencil in the right-angle corner as carefully as possible and construct a square within. Draw a diagonal through A-B.

Positioning your pencil compass at an arbitrary point along this

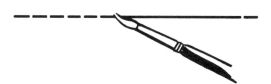

Fig. 174 To make dashes, draw a continuous line and paint out the spaces in between. It helps to draw a dash at the beginning and at the end of the line before indicating the others.

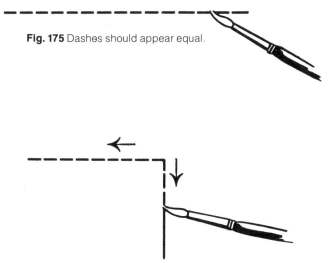

Fig. 175 Dashes should appear equal.

Fig. 176 Working from left to right, draw two lines to indicate the corner.

Fig. 177 Drawing the dashes freehand often produces uneven results.

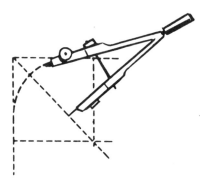

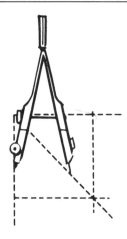

Fig. 178 To round corners, first draw a diagonal line through the right angle.

Fig. 179 Position one end of the compass on the diagonal line, the other on the edge of the square.

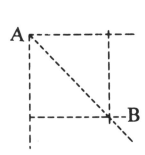

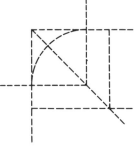

Fig. 180 Draw the curve with the compass, being sure that it blends with the straight lines.

Fig. 181 Construct a light vertical line, intersecting the circle.

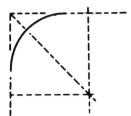

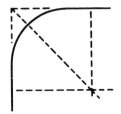

Fig. 182 Ink in the curved lines first. Do not continue the inked line beyond the intersection.

Fig. 183 Draw the straight lines to or from the curved lines.

diagonal line, open until it touches the edge, and scribe a circle (Figs. 179 and 180). Repeat this, repositioning the point along the diagonal line until the desired curve is obtained. Using the same method, construct a diagonal line in each corner. Then, with the same compass setting, move the point of the compass along the diagonal line until the pencil point touches one side. Scribe the circle. Repeat this for each corner.

Now align your T-square with the center point and draw a light horizontal line from this point, intersecting the circle. With your triangle against the T-square and lined up with the center point, construct a light vertical line, intersecting the circle (Fig. 181).

Once the corners have been thus penciled, proceed to ink in—but ink in the curved lines first (Fig. 182), using the guide lines (Fig. 181) for the limit of the curve. It is easier to draw a straight line into or from a curve than to draw a curve into or from a straight line (Fig. 183).

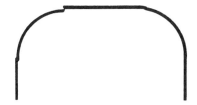

Fig. 184 Bad corner, due to inaccurate penciling.

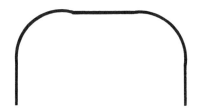

Fig. 185 Bad corner results from impatience.

Fig. 186 Inaccurate inking produces bad corners.

Although your penciling is worked out with a T-square and triangle, do not depend on these tools for the inking. There are many reasons why the lines may not match at the final inking. For one, the hole in the paper created by the compass point may widen, producing a broader swing of the compass; or, your hand may twist slightly while drawing the straight lines. Simply take a straightedge (triangle) and visually line it up so that the point of your pen (poise your pen in position slightly away from the surface) lines up with the intersection of the curve at both ends. Then ink in the line. If the line does not fall precisely on the pencil line but blends into the curve, it will not be noticed.

There are many tricks and gimmicks you can use, such as using the rounded corners supplied on adhesive-backed film. But we're concerned here with quality and the development of professional skills.

TRANSFER PAPER

The transfer sheet (or tracing sheet) is an aid to the artist for transferring shapes and drawings in the preparation of art and mechanicals. Ready-made sheets of various colors are available. However, you may prefer to prepare your own. Follow these directions:

Tape a sheet of tracing tissue onto the back of a pad (Fig. 187). Using a piece of pastel or graphite, rub from side to side, covering the entire sheet. Do not remove the excess pastel (Fig. 188).

With a ball of cotton (wet with thinner) smear neatly and lightly from side to side and top to bottom; rewet if it dries out, but do not saturate the cotton (Fig. 189).

Repeat the steps illustrated in Figs. 188 and 189 two or three times until a good coating is obtained. Test the transfer sheet by placing a piece of paper over it and tracing a line. If the traced line on the back of this piece of paper is too light, give it another coat. Cut the tissue away from the cardboard, leaving about ½" of the tape on the tissue. This will provide the paper with a protective edge.

FRENCH CURVE

Connecting curved lines requires precision and practice. The following is done if you are using a ruling pen when a technical-type pen is not available.

First, pencil in the curves accurately with your French curve. When ready to ink in, adjust the French curve until it is placed in the exact position of the pencil line. Then pull slightly away from the pencil line, keeping a parallel gap between the pencil line and the edge of the French curve. In placing the ruling pen against the French curve, this little gap will dictate the *slight* backward tilt of the pen necessary for the point to touch the pencil line, thus creating the triangular space needed to avoid

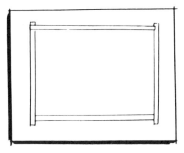

Fig. 187 To make transfer paper, first tape a sheet of tracing tissue onto the back of a pad. The tissue must be flat.

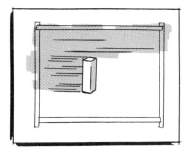

Fig. 188 Without tearing the tissue, rub a piece of pastel or graphite from side to side until you cover the sheet.

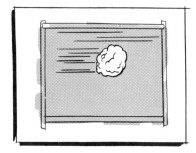

Fig. 189 Using a ball of cotton, wet with thinner, smear the surface lightly from side to side. Do not saturate the cotton.

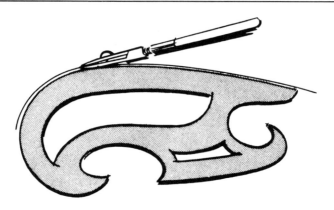

Fig. 190 As you follow the pencil line with your ruling pen, pull the pen slightly away from the pencil line, keeping a parallel gap between the pencil line and the edge of the French curve.

pulling the ink under the French curve and smearing (Fig. 190). A technical pen is better suited for working with the French curve.

If your French curve has a beveled edge, the tilt-back is not necessary. As an extra precaution, you might try placing strips of tape on the underside of the French curve, raising it from the surface and lessening the danger of blotching. With the French curve properly positioned, check visually, lining up the pen with the beginning of the curve and its intersection with the next. Then ink in the first curve. Now line up the French curve with the connecting line.

At the beginning of the connecting line, position the point above the paper and slightly to the left. Then, with a sweeping motion, bring the pen into contact with the paper, blending one line into the other. At the end or beginning of any ink line do not hold the pen in position. Learn to bring it *down* and *up* in a sweeping motion; otherwise, a ball of ink will form at the end of the line. If this should happen, you can, of course, clean it with poster paint (Figs. 191, 192, 193, and 194).

BLACKENING EDGES
To blacken edges, some artists use a black grease crayon, a felt-tip pen, or a marker. However, when cleaning with a pickup or applying thinner, they may smear, so use these with discretion.

Black ink or paint, applied with a crowquill or brush, is generally used for this purpose. The edges should be blackened before cementing into position. Blackening in after the piece has been cemented into position is both risky and troublesome. It is not always easy to clean the cement completely from the edge, which makes it difficult to apply the ink or paint.

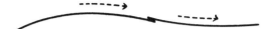

Fig. 191 If two lines do not connect, as shown here, it is impossible to repair and must be done over.

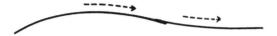

Fig. 192 This is a common error, difficult to repair.

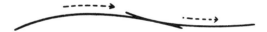

Fig. 193 This is a good intersection, but the lines are drawn too far. Clean with white paint.

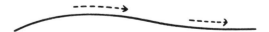

Fig. 194 Connecting lines should look like this.

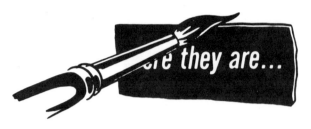

Fig. 195 When blackening edges, do not hold the art work facing toward you.

Fig. 196 Hold the art facing away from the brush, as shown here.

A word of caution: use an old brush for blackening, because the sharpness of the paper edge will cut the hair on the brush. You may also slip and damage the art if the cut edge is very close. The safest and surest way is to hold the piece with the live matter facing away from the brush (Figs. 195 and 196). If you should slip, you will not impair the art. However, ink or paint may be cleaned off a photostat or photograph if it is wiped immediately with water and cotton.

BLACK AREAS
For large areas of black on the mechanical or overlay, black paper is a time saver. First, ink in a clean outline and build up about ¼" width (Fig. 197). Then cut a sheet of black paper to a size within that ¼", blacken the edges, and cement into the area (Fig. 198).

This will give complete coverage of the area with clean and accurate edges. It isn't always advisable to use the cut edge of the colored paper as the actual edge, for the simple reason that it may chip or peel. However, use the method you find best suited to the requirements of the layout.

In areas not large enough to bother using black paper, you may try filling in with black poster paint. Black paint dries in an even, flat black; it looks neater than ink and is better for reproduction. Additionally, rubber cement may be picked up with ease from a painted area, whereas cement has a tendency to adhere very firmly to ink, making it difficult to pick up. One word in the defense of ink—it is easier to touch up with white paint. Black paint does not work out too well on acetate—it has a tendency to crack and peel off, but it may be used in an emergency.

Here is a bit of advice: avoid using black marker on your mechanicals—for any reason. If you should apply cement or thinner to it, it will run, leaving a stain impossible to remove.

Red adhesive-backed film is a great material for preparing solid shapes. It can be conveniently placed over your pencil drawing and cut to the shape. Peel away the unwanted areas, and you're left with a red silhouette of the shape. This can either be used as it is for reproduction, or a photostat can be made from it, producing a black shape to be used as art. Cutting this material produces very sharp corners, probably sharper than one could ink. This is an extremely useful material.

Fig. 197 To cover large areas of black on a mechanical or overlay, first ink in a clean outline, about ¼" wide.

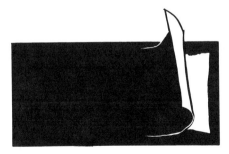

Fig. 198 Then drop cement down a sheet of black paper to a size within that area and blacken the edges.

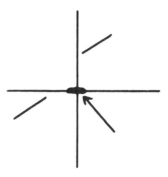

Fig. 199 If the colored line is drawn first, the black will run into it and spread.

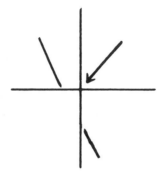

Fig. 200 However, if the black line is drawn first, a clean joint will result.

COLORED LINES

Lines that crisscross will spread slightly at the intersection. In lines of the same color this may not be too serious. On the other hand, where black and blue or red lines intersect, the black will run into the colored line if the colored line is drawn first (Fig. 199). If the black line is drawn, then the colored line, a clean joint will result (Fig. 200).

A most effective method when ruling colored lines is using poster paint rather than ink. Dilute the paint to a consistency that will permit it to flow freely from the pen. It will dry an even color and can be drawn over another color without a "see-through."

MOUNTING BUCKLED PHOTOS

Photos that are slightly curled or wrinkled can be mounted in the following manner. Cement both surfaces and allow them to dry. Using both hands, hold the photo at either end and bend the sides together (Fig. 201).

Place the curved edge onto the cemented board. *Roll* one side down (keeping the thumb pressed on the upper surface to prevent buckling) and lightly burnish with the hand outward from the center (Fig. 202). Repeat with the other side.

Place a tissue over the photo and burnish outward from the center, forcing out the air creases. Rather than use the slipsheet method, this is also a quick method for mounting a photo that is not wrinkled but does not have to be placed accurately into position. If the edges persistently buckle and pull up, you could use a strip of white masking tape to hold them down.

Photos that are severely buckled or wrinkled present a difficult problem. If you aren't extremely careful, you can make it worse. Probably your

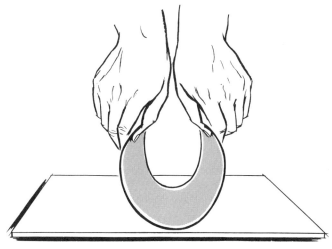

Fig. 201 To mount a curled or wrinkled photo, first hold the photo at either end and bend the edges together.

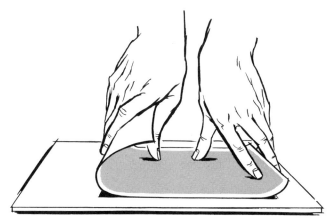

Fig. 202 Roll down one side, keeping the thumbs pressed on the upper surface of the photo to prevent buckling.

best solution is to send it to your stat house or photo lab and have them rewash and dry it. In most instances this should work. Do not attempt to do this yourself unless you have the proper equipment; you could easily ruin the print.

Of course, if the photo contains retouching you cannot use this approach. It may be best simply to tack it down at the corners with tape.

CUTTING

Whenever possible, cut along the outside edge of the needed piece. If the blade should slip, it will cut into the excess and not damage the area you are cutting out (Figs. 203 and 204).

In cutting a heavy board (illustration board), it is not necessary to apply too much pressure on the blade or knife in an attempt to cut through in one stroke. This is dangerous and usually produces an irregular edge. A few strokes of the blade, with even pressure, will produce a clean, even cut. *Caution*: always use a steel ruler as a cutting guide. It is not advisable to use a soft metal (such as aluminum) ruler, least of all a wooden ruler, as a cutting edge. The blade can easily grip the edge and slide off its path, possibly causing serious injury.

Whenever possible, cut along the right-hand edge of the ruler. Never position yourself in such a way that you are crisscrossing hands while cutting. Besides making proper cutting difficult, it is obviously dangerous. If you are left-handed, you should cut along the left side of the ruler.

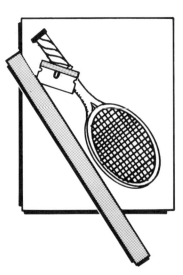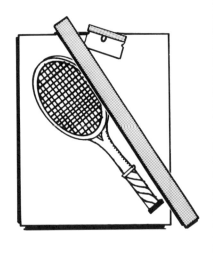

Fig. 203 Do not cut art with the razor blade on the side of the art.

Fig. 204 Always cut with the blade on the side away from the art.

CUTTING AND BUTTING

Here is a simple approach for butting or notching two or more elements, such as photos or colored paper (photos in this example).

The layout (Fig. 205) indicates that photo B is to notch into photo A. B and C are to butt flush. After assuring yourself that each photo will fit its respective shape, very carefully pencil in the shapes on the board.

Tape a tissue over the board and trace an accurate outline of the shapes. At this stage, you may also *lightly* trace the elements of each photo onto the tissue in proper position as a guide for pasting up and cropping. Use a *soft pencil* or felt-tip pen for tracing over photos. Apply only light pressure or you may score the surface of the photo.

Cement photo A and, while it is still wet, place it in position beneath the tissue, lining up the photo with the tracing. You may use the dry slipsheet method if you prefer (Fig. 206).

Cut lines 1-2, 2-3 (Fig. 207). Do not attempt to cut out the notched area of photo A. Now paste up photo C in the same manner as A. Do not cut at this stage (Fig. 208).

Cement photo B into position overlapping A and C (Fig. 209). Double check to be certain that all edges overlap enough to ensure clean butting after cutting. With a push pin, lightly pinpoint all the corners through the tissue and photos (Fig. 210). Lift the tissue and, with a steel straightedge and a sharp razor blade, line up the pinpoints and cut through both layers of photos (Fig. 211). In cutting, approach the corners with care. Do not cut

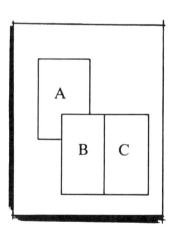

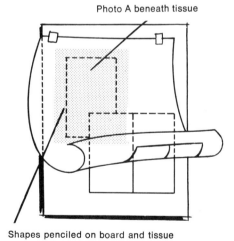

Photo A beneath tissue

Shapes penciled on board and tissue

Fig. 205 Here is the layout: photo *B* is to notch into photo *A*. *B* and *C* are to butt flush.

Fig. 206 After tracing an accurate outline of the shapes, cement photo *A* under the tissue, lining it up with the tracing.

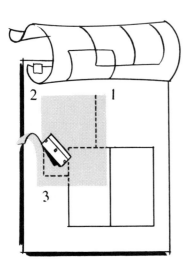

Fig. 207 Cut out the lines, without cutting out the notched area of the photo.

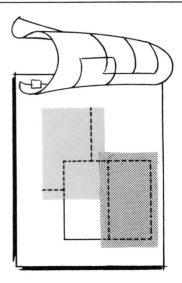

Fig. 208 Paste up photo *C* in the same manner. Do not cut tissue.

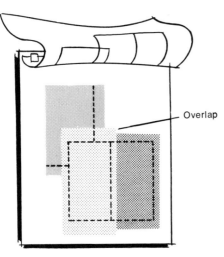

Fig. 209 Cement photo *B* into position, overlapping *A* and *C*.

Overlap

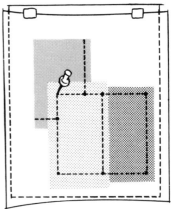

Fig. 210 Lightly pinpoint all the corners through the tissue and photos.

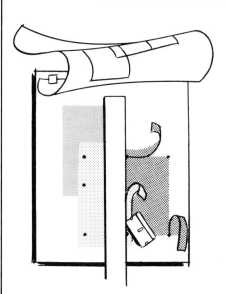

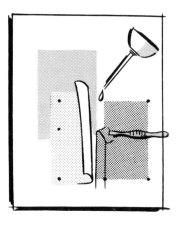

Fig. 211 After lifting the tissue, line up the pinpoints with a straightedge and cut through both layers of photos.

Fig. 212 Lift overlay, wet down the piece beneath it with thinner.

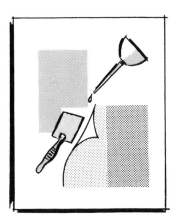

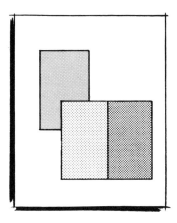

Fig. 213 Pull out the piece. Be careful not to crack the photo when lifting the corner.

Fig. 214 Clean up excess rubber cement. Check edges for clean cuts and butting.

beyond the corners, for the cut marks may mar the surrounding area.

Discard excess areas. Lift the remaining overlap, wet down the piece beneath it with thinner, and pull it out, dropping the overlap back into position (Figs. 212 and 213). Clean up excess rubber cement, rubbing *away* from the edges. Never erase or pickup in a direction toward the edge of the cemented piece or you might tear it (Fig. 214).

Another method employed by some artists is to eliminate the pinpointing and cut directly through the tracing and photos simultaneously.

STRIPPING ILLUSTRATION BOARD

The surface of illustration board can be stripped from its cardboard backing, making it possible to effect changes in art, i.e., to transfer art to other surfaces without the thick backing or to gang up two or more pieces of art onto one board.

At a corner of the board, lift the surface away from the backing with a razor blade and pull it up about 1" (Fig. 215). Place a clean wide cardboard cylinder diagonally across the lifted corner. Gripping the cylinder with both hands, press the loosened corner against the cylinder with the thumbs (Fig. 216).

Then roll the cylinder slowly and carefully until the entire piece is wrapped around it. Unroll it and, holding it face up at both ends, slide it lightly back and forth along the edge of your drawing table or any suitable smooth edge. This will relieve the piece of its curl (Fig. 217).

Before cementing a stripped piece, sand down the back to prevent impressions from showing through the surface. Press the paper firmly with a free hand while sanding to prevent creasing or tearing. When sanding edges, sand out from the edge, being careful not to nick it. *Caution:* should the back of the surface begin to show while sanding—stop! You may cut through the surface.

The surface can be stripped without the use of a cylinder (especially small pieces). The trick is to keep the piece taut while pulling. Do not roll it or bend it in the direction in which you are stripping.

USING GLUE

Pasting up small or tiny pieces of type, such as a number, a single letter, or patching a misspelled word, is common practice in preparing mechanicals. The biggest problem is getting these small pieces to adhere firmly. If you use ordinary rubber cement, the piece generally picks up when you remove the excess cement. This is especially true and rather disconcerting when working on acetate. While one-coat cement is probably the most practical, try using a dab of white or clear water-soluble glue instead of rubber cement. The glue can be applied with the point of a pencil.

In preparing involved dummies, such as boxes or displays that require

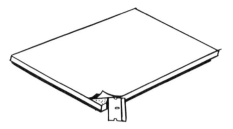

Fig. 215 To strip illustration board, lift the surface away at the corner.

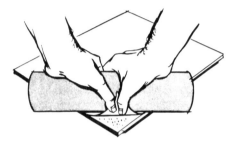

Fig. 216 Grip a cardboard cylinder with both hands and press the loosened corner against the cylinder with the thumbs.

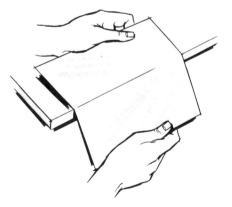

Fig. 217 After rolling the cylinder until the entire piece is wrapped around it, slide the piece along the edge of the table.

tabs and flaps, glue is much more satisfactory than rubber cement. Excess water-soluble glue can be cleaned with a piece of damp cloth or cotton.

Mix a dab of this glue with your water paint. It is excellent for painting on difficult or slick surfaces that may repel the water paint.

A word of advice: do not use glue or paste to mount photos. After drying, it pulls the print surface into sunken impressions, possibly ruining the photo.

PREPARING LINE ART

If you are handling a complete job, illustration as well as mechanical, and you must prepare a line drawing, try drawing the art *repro size* if possible. The advantage here is that you will save time by not having to bother with photostats; the reproduction will be better because the art will be shot directly instead of from a stat; you will have better control in positioning it by working with it same size.

Familiarization with materials and tools in conjunction with an understanding of reproduction is most important in your development as a professional. It leads to shortcuts, better results, and creativity. But when you prepare line art, do not be confused with gimmicks as the answer to your problems. Gimmicks often disguise themselves as the best way to do something because it is faster or easier, but they usually stunt your development. There is nothing wrong with finding a shortcut or an easier way to produce a result, but do not lose sight of the fact that gimmicks, like drugs, only delude you into thinking that you are developing. Learn the difference between a mere trick and a legitimate solution.

The following exercises can be used as typical examples of what may frustrate the artist into using a gimmick, but these gimmicks prevent him or her from developing a skill necessary to produce a quality product. Before attempting these exercises, let's consider the possible approaches.

THE STAR

Suppose you had to produce a solid black or solid-color star.

Gimmick: find a picture of a star, have a negative photostat made to a larger size than required for reproduction, and, with black and white ink or paint, clean it up. Have a positive stat made to correct size.

This serves the purpose, has limited use, and has not developed your ability. Suppose you had to produce the star in color? What would you do? Color the photostat? This may very well require the skill you have lacked in the first place.

Another gimmick would be to construct the star on black or colored paper and cut it out. You will get quick results, but this method often produces frayed edges and poor reproduction, which are difficult to repair. These methods may help in the preparation of dummies and such, but they do not mature your skills.

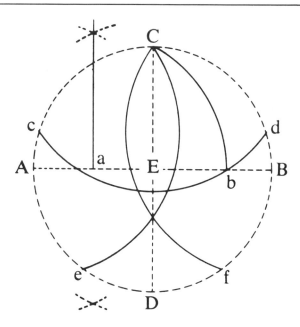

Fig. 218 Divide the circumference of a circle into four equal parts: *A, B, C,* and *D*. Label the center point *E*. Then divide *A E* in half (point *a*); place the compass on point *a* and, opening it to *C*, draw arc *Cb* (*b* intersecting line *EB*). Then place the compass on point *C* and, extending it to the intersection *b*, scribe arc *cbd*. With the compass placed at *c* and extended to *C*, scribe arc *Ce*; then place the compass on point *d*, extending it to *C*, and draw *Cf*.

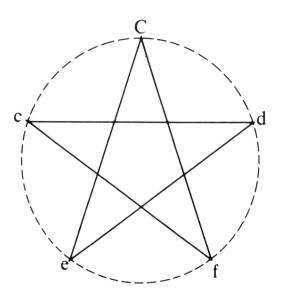

Fig. 219 Now connect *Ce, Cf, cd, cf, de*.

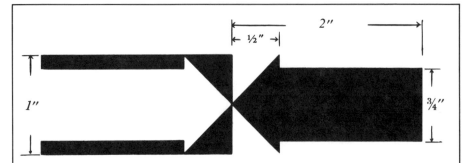

Fig. 220 Construct the above arrows following instructions as indicated. Keep the corners clean and sharp. Here is where your brush and ruler will be useful. Before inking, make a clean, accurate drawing. Notice what occurs at the meeting point of the two arrows after inking. Red adhesive film would be ideal for this, but try inking it.

PROFESSIONAL APPROACH

Construct the star in pencil (Fig. 218). Ink it in with a ruling or technical pen (Fig. 219).

If you have to produce a star in color, try using colored paint in your ruling pen. But, then again, you must know how to use the ruling pen.

Perhaps the best approach would be one really using ingenuity (not a gimmick): construct the star in pencil. Cover the entire art with a piece of red adhesive color film (page 79). Then carefully cut along the edges and remove the excess. The result will be far superior to any other method. The corners and points will be sharp and clean. The entire shape will be flat, with no danger of the edges fraying unless it is mishandled.

If you should fault during the performance, you can simply remove the film and start over or patch the area. The red color film will reproduce as if it were black ink.

If you had to construct a colored star, you would, of course, use that particular color of film.

Also study the arrows, Fig. 220.

The geometric formula in Fig. 218 is best used as an exercise for the development of your skills. A more direct approach would be to use an adjustable triangle or protractor. Simply mark off every 72° around the circumference and connect the points as in Fig. 219.

THE GRID

Now construct a grid. Gimmick: pencil the exercise as shown (Fig. 221). Use black and red tapes instead of ink. This method is fast but not professional, and it develops nothing for you. Of course, it is fine for presentations, layouts, dummies, and such, but we are concerned here with top-quality mechanical preparation for reproduction. You'll also find this method can be more frustrating than if you had inked it in. It may be

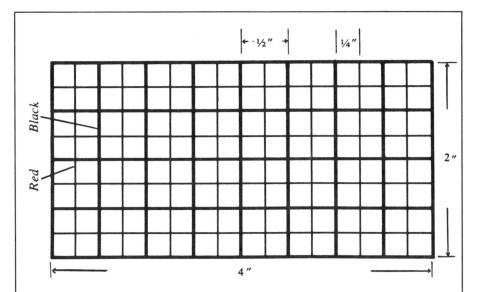

Fig. 221 The illustration above is your layout. Follow it accurately. Be careful at the intersections—draw the black lines first. Follow the layout for thicknesses of lines. Measure accurately and pencil in before inking. Heavy lines are black; thin lines are red.

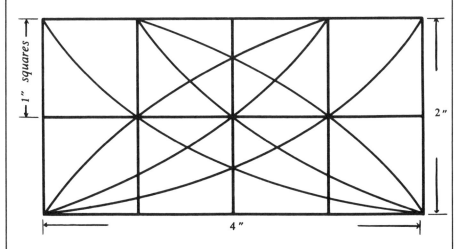

Fig. 222 Your finished piece should look exactly like the layout above. The intersections must be precisely as shown.

more difficult to get the tape straight than you might imagine. The crisscrosses and overlaps often produce poor results in reproduction.

Use a ruling or a technical pen for the black lines. Mix red paint so that it will flow freely from your ruling pen and proceed to rule the red lines directly over the black. The red paint should block out the black line beneath it, creating a three-dimensional illustration. This requires skill and can be used for similar projects. Also study the French curve, Fig. 222.

There are, of course, other possibilities, but those just described may serve as a guide. Make an earnest attempt to do these exercises professionally.

These exercises have been designed specifically to develop your manual skills. If you can master them, you will be well on your way toward being a professional.

CHAPTER 8

PROPORTIONAL SCALING

W<small>HEN ART</small> (photo, drawing, etc.) is not the actual size for reproduction and a lucy machine (projection camera) is not available, a scaling method may be employed to determine whether or not the art will fit the specifications (when reduced or enlarged) indicated in the layout.

Proportional scaling simply means that a shape, when reduced or enlarged in height, will proportionately reduce or enlarge in width, and vice versa. If we enlarge the 5″ side of a 5″ × 10″ rectangle to 15″ (3 times); then the 10″ side should increase in proportion—10″ × 3 = 30″—with a total result of 15″ × 30″.

With the simple figures just described there is no problem. Nevertheless, there are times when the proportion of increase is not so easily ascertained. By using the method about to be described, you will have not only an accurate size, but also a quick visual of the shape in its new size, enabling you to change it immediately to suit your need without arithmetic or even a ruler.

DIAGONAL SCALING

There are occasions when there is no time to shoot a stat of the art to the desired size, or there may be so many pieces to be done that it would be impractical to shoot stats for a low-budget job. In addition to scaling art, you will have to scale mechanicals to fit different page sizes. Each publication, newspaper, etc., has its own column and page size. If, for example, the client is running an ad in four different newspapers throughout the country, your mechanical should be prepared in scale to fit each of these specifications, or else a separate mechanical must be made for each size.

In scaling a rectangle or square, draw a diagonal line through *AB* (Fig.

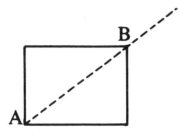

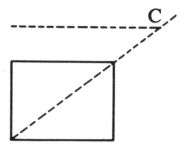

Fig. 223 In scaling a rectangle or a square, draw a diagonal line through *AB*.

Fig. 224 Draw desired height as a horizontal line to intersect with diagonal.

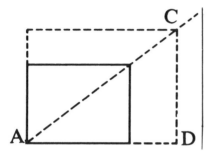

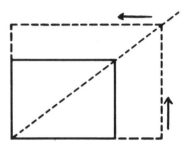

Fig. 225 From the intersection, drop a line to the extended base *AD*.

Fig. 226 Where the width is known, reverse the procedure.

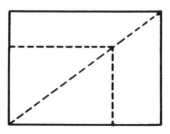

Fig. 227 With reduction, use the same procedure, working within the shape.

223). In enlargements where desired height is known, mark off the height and draw a horizontal line from that point across until it meets the diagonal line (point C). This is, of course, an arbitrary point depending upon the height (Fig. 224). Drop a vertical line from that point to the extended base line AD. This will give you the width, at that height, in proportion (Fig. 225).

If enlargement on width is known, draw a vertical from that point to the diagonal and a horizontal across the intersection (Fig. 226). If reduction is required, the same procedure is employed, working within the shape (Fig. 227).

Drawing the above on a tissue and placing it over the art will afford you an excellent visual aid in determining where the art may be cropped.

SCALING IRREGULAR SHAPES
Construct a square or rectangle around the extremes of the shape (Figs. 228 and 229). Draw an infinite diagonal line through AB. Determine the overall size required and follow the instructions above ("Diagonal Scaling") to construct the square or rectangle, containing the original shape, in proportion (Fig. 230).

A diagonal line may be drawn from A through any point falling along lines FB, BG in order to project it to the determined size (AECD). In this case, the only point falling along FB is a. Draw Aaa1 (Fig. 231). Point b falls on BG. Draw line Abb1.

To draw a diagonal line through a point *not* on line FB or BG in itself would conclude nothing. Two aspects of that point must be taken into consideration: its relative height and its relative position at that height.

Points c and d exist in space a certain distance up from AG and a certain distance in from BG. If you transfer c to line BG (c1) by drawing a horizontal through that point, you will have a point through which you may draw a diagonal line to CD (Fig. 232). Point c2 represents the height of c in scale to AECD. Repeat the same for d.

Draw a diagonal line through points c and d. Now draw a horizontal line across from c2 and d2 until it meets the diagonal just drawn. At their intersection you will find c3, or c in its relative position; and d3, or d in its relative position in scale (Fig. 233).

Any point along AF or AG must be transferred to its opposite line BG or FB. Therefore, a perpendicular from points e and f to line FB must be drawn, thus setting up points e1 and f1, through which you may draw a diagonal to line EC (Fig. 234).

Now, simply drop e2 and f2 to line AD (Fig. 235). Points e3 and f3 now represent e and f in the same relative position in scale to AECD. Connect all plotted points (Fig. 236).

Remember: all diagonal lines must be drawn from A through a point existing in space and/or through a point only on lines FB or BG.

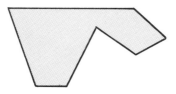

Fig. 228 The problem is to scale this irregular shape.

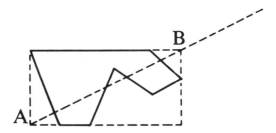

Fig. 229 Construct a square or rectangle around the extremes of the shape.

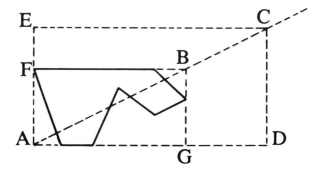

Fig. 230 Enlarge the overall size in the same way you would a square or rectangle.

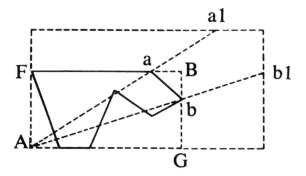

Fig. 231 Projecting and establishing line *ab*.

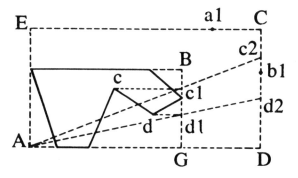

Fig. 232 Projecting line *cd*.

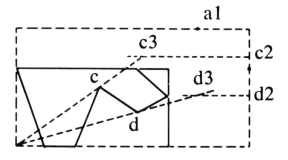

Fig. 233 Establishing *cd*.

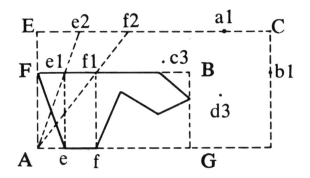

Fig. 234 Projecting line *ef*.

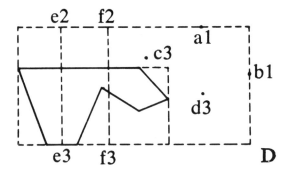

Fig. 235 Establishing line *ef*.

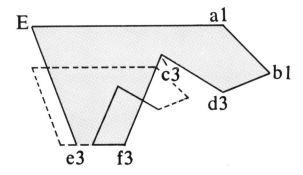

Fig. 236 Here is the new size in proportion.

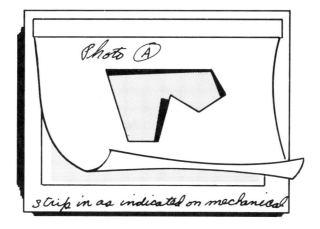

Fig. 237 A mask can be used to indicate a new size when photostats are not available.

Now and then the layout will consist of many photos or art (as in a catalog, brochure, etc.). The cost of statting many photos may be too high for the job. Therefore, by using the diagonal system, you will be able to re-create the shape proportionately to any size larger or smaller to accommodate the original art. Once the size and shape are ascertained, cut it out of a sheet of heavy bond, place it over the art in proper position, and tape it across the top. This is called a "mask" (Fig. 237).

On the mechanical, the actual shape (reproduction size) is drawn in a blue line and keyed (*AB*, etc.) to correspond with the art. The masked art will present an excellent visual of how the art fits into that particular shape. Needless to say, you may have limited use for this type of projection. It is described here more for the sake of exercising your skills. But you never know when you may need to use it. It makes excellent practice, which is what you may need at this point.

EXERCISE
Trace the shape in Fig. 238 and enlarge it proportionately from height *A* to height *B*. Using different colored pencils for identification of plotting lines may simplify this procedure. After having drawn the shape to its new size, try cutting it out of a piece of heavy bond.

There will be occasions when you will have to cut a mask for a photo or art to correspond in proportion to a particular shape in a layout. By applying the principles just covered, you will be able to plot any shape to any size, larger or smaller, in correct proportion.

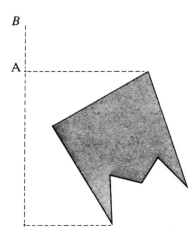

Fig. 238 Enlarge this shape proportionately from height *A* to height *B*.

PROPORTION SCALE WHEEL

For simple shapes (triangle, square, etc.) that must be enlarged considerably (as in posters, presentations, etc.) and where the diagonal line system is physically impractical, the fastest and surest method is to use a proportion circular scale wheel.

For example, if the original art measures 7″ wide by 10″ high and it must be enlarged to 40″ high, you must be concerned with how wide it will have to be at this height to be in proportion. Since the height must be increased four times, the solution is simple: multiply the width (7″) by 4 = 28″. So, the overall size would be 28″ by 40″. But should the measurements be uneven numbers—7³⁄₁₆″ × 10⁵⁄₈″—and the enlargement an odd size—37¹⁵⁄₁₆″—the percentage of enlargement becomes more difficult to ascertain. Therefore, the scale wheel should be used and is extremely handy. Instructions for its use are clearly indicated on the instrument. The mathematical formula for proportion:

Width is to width as height is to height, i.e., $\dfrac{7''}{x} = \dfrac{10''}{40''} = \dfrac{28''}{10x\sqrt{280}}$

SPACE DIVISION

How to divide odd-sized areas into equal spaces is an important thing to know, especially in the preparation of charts and graphs. A fast and accurate system is, once again, the principle of the diagonal approach.

As an example, we will use an area 7³⁄₁₆″ wide by 3⅛″ high. The width is to be divided into six equal spaces, the height into five. In order to divide the height into five equal spaces, first pencil in the overall shape.

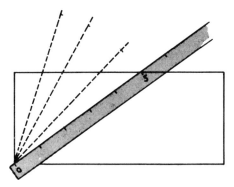

Fig. 239 To divide odd-sized areas into five equal spaces: first pivot the ruler from the lower left-hand corner until the 5″ mark touches the top horizontal line.

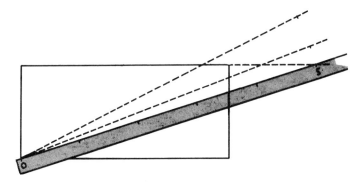

Fig. 240 If necessary, extend the top line to meet the 5″ mark.

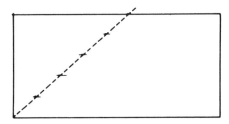

Fig. 241 Draw a diagonal and divide that diagonal into five equal points.

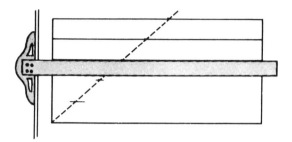

Fig. 242 Using your T-square, draw five horizontal lines.

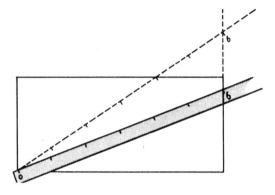

Fig. 243 To divide the width into six equal parts, pivot the ruler along the opposite vertical.

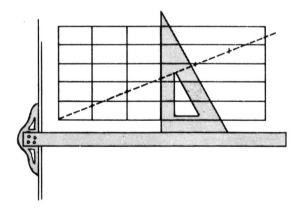

Fig. 244 Drawing vertical lines through the points, follow the same procedure as before.

Place the 0 mark of your ruler at the lower left-hand corner. Pivoting the ruler at this point, swing it until the 5″ mark touchs the *top horizontal line* (Fig. 239).

If the 5″ mark goes beyond the original shape, simply extend the top line and swing the ruler until it meets it (Fig. 240). If the 5″ mark does not reach the top line, i.e., if the space is too wide, calculate an equal multiple of 5″ that will reach it—10″, for example, counting every other inch as one.

Once the diagonal position has been attained, hold your ruler firmly and draw a light line along the edge. Now, ruler still in place, mark off the five equal points (Fig. 241). Draw a *horizontal* line through each point with your T-square (Fig. 242).

In order to determine the division of the *width*, place the end of your ruler in the lower left-hand corner and pivot it until the 6″ mark touches the *opposite vertical* (Fig. 243).

Follow the same procedure as just described for the height, with one exception: draw *vertical* lines through the points (Fig. 244).

This is one of the methods used in plotting charts and graphs, as well as preparing mechanicals that need particular spacing of shapes and areas. A helpful device in calculating spaces is the engineer's scale rule.

EXERCISE
Divide a rectangle 8⅝″ wide by 4¹³⁄₁₆″ high into 10 equal horizontal spaces and 13 equal vertical spaces (Fig. 245).

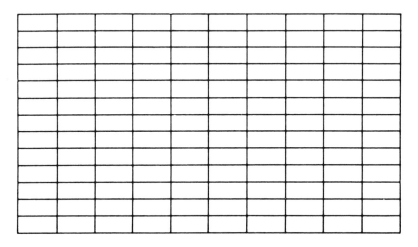

Fig. 245 Divide a rectangle in this proportion into 10 equal horizontal spaces and 13 equal vertical spaces.

CONSIDERING THE TIME FACTOR

One important aspect of advertising should not be overlooked: the element of time. As a general rule, a job should be completed as quickly as possible. On many occasions, there is very little time in which to execute a mechanical. Time sheets or some other sort of record are accurately kept of the work entailed during a project. This system is not necessarily employed to check on the artist's capabilities, but as a means of estimating the cost for billing the client.

Obviously, the faster the artist, the more valuable he or she becomes to the organization. But do not overlook the fact that speed comes from knowledge and experience. Working fast, without forethought, may result in a mass of confusion and errors, jeopardizing the reputation of the agency or studio *as well as your position*.

Rather than rush frantically and furiously into a mechanical, simply study its requirements. Then decide how you should approach its execution. If you know the information covered in this book, the performance will not take any longer than is necessary.

CHAPTER 9

HOW TO EXECUTE A MECHANICAL

Eᴀᴄʜ ʟᴀʏᴏᴜᴛ has its own significant characteristics. The approach and method of preparing a mechanical are relative to these characteristics and to the different working procedures in each agency and studio. In order to prepare a mechanical easily and efficiently, it is necessary not only to understand the information just covered, but also to develop an approach to its analysis and execution. Because of this, there is no rule of approach. Each artist has a particular way of handling a mechanical; nevertheless, I have outlined here a general approach applicable to most situations through which you may develop your own methods.

STEP ONE
Analyze the layout or dummy and *ask questions*. Never start a mechanical without having a thorough understanding of its requirements:

(a) How is it to be used—as a mailing piece, newspaper ad, magazine page, etc.?

(b) A black and white job, two-color, or multicolor?

(c) Any halftones (art or photos)?

(d) What size is the mechanical to be? Any bleed areas or folds?

(e) If die cutting is involved, check the shape.

(f) Does the type fit the layout?

(g) Will you need photostats or Veloxes? Any silhouetting?

(h) Reverse copy? Surprint?

(i) If screen tints or color separation is needed, what method is to be used—keyline, solid black on board, overlays, color film sheet?

(j) How much time is available?

Once these questions have been resolved by your art director, production manager, or supervisor, you may start the mechanical.

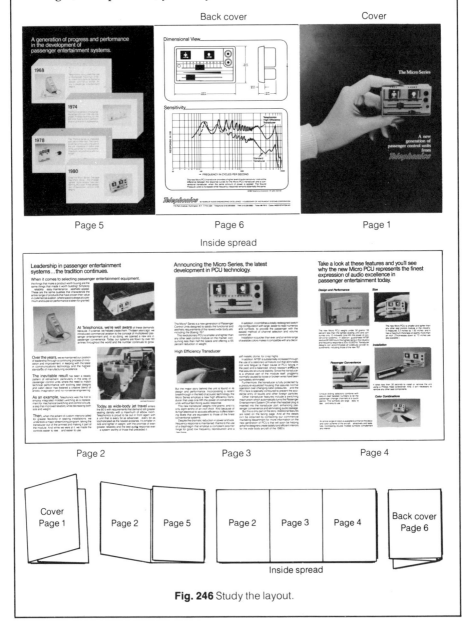

Fig. 246 Study the layout.

STEP TWO

If the type proof you are working with is machine set, it must be fixed to prevent smearing (Fig. 247). If the type is photo composed, there is no need to fix it. Most artists prefer to cement the back of the entire proof (Fig. 248), allow it to dry, place it (back down) onto the cutting mat, and cut out all the type areas with a razor blade and steel T-square, leaving them in place on the mat (Fig. 249). Then, as each piece is needed, it is lifted and used.

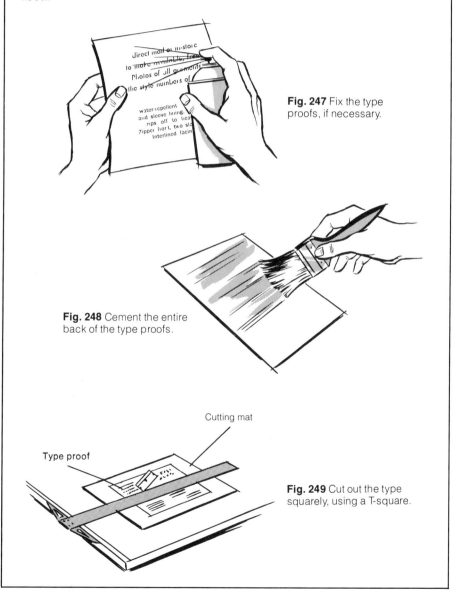

Fig. 247 Fix the type proofs, if necessary.

Fig. 248 Cement the entire back of the type proofs.

Cutting mat

Type proof

Fig. 249 Cut out the type squarely, using a T-square.

This method, of course, is the most practical because it minimizes handling of the type, keeps the cemented area clean, and produces a neater cutting job. It also prevents cement from wetting and smearing the type, which would occur if pieces were individually cut and then cemented.

Never cut with a good plastic T-square or triangle; one nick will ruin its efficiency for inking work. If a steel triangle is not available, keep on hand a particular triangle to be used just for cutting. Aluminum or magnesium tools are dangerous for cutting. They are too soft; the blade often catches and rides up.

It may be worthwhile to investigate the usefulness of other types of more modern and effective true edges.

STEP THREE

As a time saver, order your stats (if any) before starting the mechanical, being certain of correct sizes. While you are preparing the mechanical, your stats are being made. If the stats are ordered after you have gone as far as you can with the execution of the mechanical, there will be a delay while you wait for them. Time is vitally important and costly in business (Fig. 250).

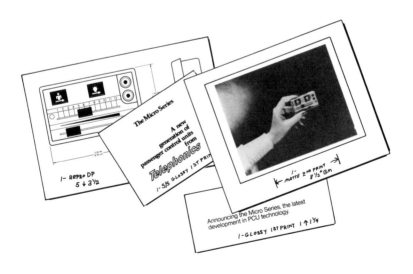

Fig. 250 Order photostats.

STEP FOUR

Set up your board. Cut the illustration board about 2" or 3" larger than the mechanical size to allow a comfortable margin for written instructions. *Never* use pebbled matboard for a mechanical. If the layout calls for any amount of inking, be certain to use a smooth surfaced illustration board for cleaner lines. Where textured effects are required in inking, use the medium or rough surfaced illustration board.

Now "square up" your board. Position your board on the left of the drawing table, being certain not to overlap the straight edge of the drawing table. This will allow some working space at your right and will afford better results in using your T-square and triangle. If you are left-handed, reverse this procedure.

Holding your T-square firmly in position at the lower portion of your drawing table, line up the bottom edge of the illustration board against it. You can tack it down at the top corners with push pins, but masking tape on all four corners may be more convenient. Be careful when removing this tape or you may strip the surface of the illustration board.

With T-square and triangle, pencil in the overall required size of the mechanical (visually centered). For most accurate and clean penciling, use a 6H or 9H pencil with a long sharp point (use your sanding block). This will minimize excess graphite smudges caused by the use of softer pencils. Do not press too hard, or you may damage the surface of the board (which, subsequently, will cause poor inking). Cleanliness and accuracy are the hallmarks of a professional mechanical.

Caution: the beginner has a tendency to dig the pencil into the board while marking off sizes. This will cause holes in the board or paper and perhaps result in a poor inking job.

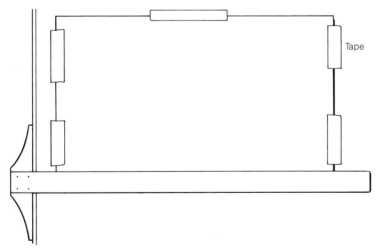

Fig. 251 Tape down the illustration board so that it is square on your drawing table.

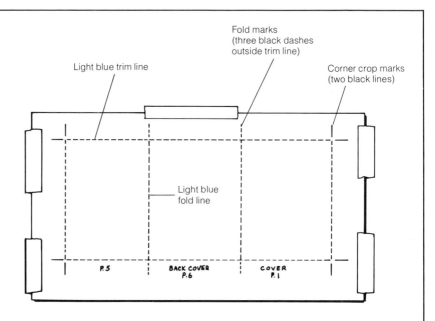

Fig. 252 Rule up the form indicating the overall trim and fold areas. Label each page for identification.

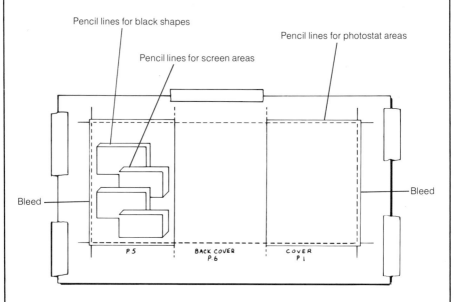

Fig. 253 Construct the shapes to be inked or screened, or to be occupied by photostats. Note: the fold and trim lines in these illustrations are indicated as dashed lines only for demonstration. In actuality, they are to be drawn as continuous lines, not dashes.

STEP FIVE

Once the overall size has been lightly penciled in, *ink in crop marks and/or fold marks* where and if required as well as fold lines and trim lines (shown as dashed lines in Figs. 252, 253, and 254, but they should be continuous light blue lines; see page 91). This will ensure the retention of sizes and areas in the event that the penciling is erased during the process of pasting up (Fig. 252). It will also serve as a means of checking, as you progress, the squareness of the mechanical. Now pencil in the entire mechanical: areas to be screened, etc. *Do not ink in yet* (Fig. 253).

STEP SIX

Check type, using the glassine on top of the mechanical and elements to be pasted in, being certain that they fit properly in accordance with the layout. Also scrutinize the type for broken letters or smears (Fig. 254).

Check sizes of shapes, photos, art, bleed areas, etc. You will often find that the elements to be assembled in the mechanical do not fit precisely as indicated in the layout. Should the difference in size be considerable, bring it to the attention of your art director or whoever is in charge of the project. He or she will suggest the necessary changes. If the difference is slight, use your own judgment in arranging the elements to resemble the layout as closely as possible. Remember, often the layout is done freehand. It merely represents the "effect" the art director has in mind.

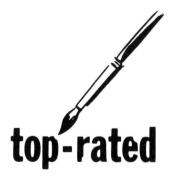

top-rated

Fig. 254 Clean broken type.

STEP SEVEN

Once these questions have been resolved, ink in the required areas (Fig. 255). If, as often occurs with the beginner, the elements are cemented in before inking, the chances of scratching, dirtying, or dropping ink onto the type or art are very likely to be increased. This may mean doing the entire mechanical over or manipulating extensively to rectify the condition; inking in before cementing in the type or art will minimize the danger to the components, if an error is encountered (spilling, blotching, wrong size, etc.). In addition to this, there is less danger of smudging or

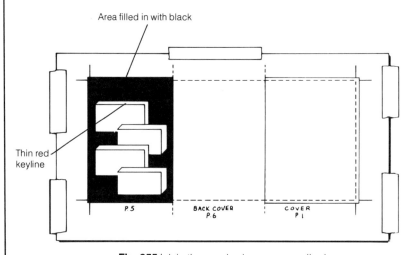

Area filled in with black

Thin red keyline

P.5   BACK COVER P.6   COVER P.1

Fig. 255 Ink in the required areas accordingly.

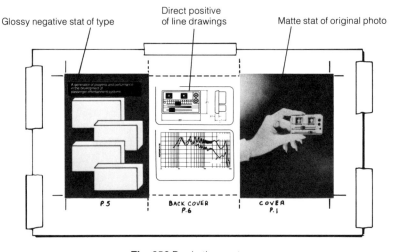

Glossy negative stat of type

Direct positive of line drawings

Matte stat of original photo

P.5   BACK COVER P.6   COVER P.1

Fig. 256 Begin the paste-up

scratching the pasted elements as a result of manipulation of the T-square and triangle. Accuracy of size, shape, and squareness of your mechanical are of prime importance.

STEP EIGHT

Commence paste-up (Fig. 256). Usually, by the time your stats arrive, a good portion (if not all) of the mechanical will have been completed. This depends upon the complexity of the job. Check the stats for proper size and positioning. If all is in order, continue the mechanical (Figs. 257 and 258).

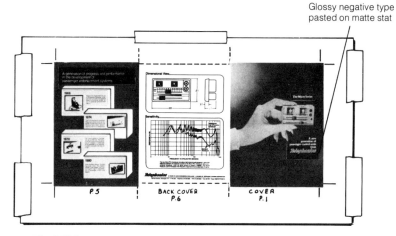

Glossy negative type pasted on matte stat

Fig. 257 Continue pasting up type. The mechanical is completed.

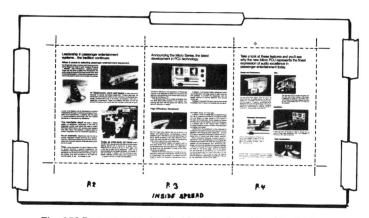

Fig. 258 Prepare a mechanical for the other side of the folder.

STEP NINE

At the completion of the job, you should double check against the dummy or layout, being certain that all elements are the correct size and in their proper position. Using red ink, "X" out each photostat of continuous tone art and indicate on the stat "For size and position only. Strip in halftone from original art." The line (glossy) stats should *not* be "X'd" out, as they would more than likely be used for finished art.

Next, pick up excess rubber cement and clean the board with a good eraser. Required instructions, sizes, job number, etc., should be written in the margin. If screen or color indications are required, tape a sheet of tracing paper across the top covering the entire board and indicate the requirements. A tracing paper or vellum cover is also convenient for written instructions or indicated changes (Fig. 259). In addition to the tissue flap, a heavier paper flap is cemented about 3" along the top of the reverse side of the board and flapped over the front for decor and protection (Fig. 260).

The mechanical, along with the dummy or layout and art, should then be presented to your supervisor for final checking (Fig. 261).

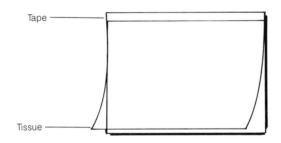

Tape

Tissue

Fig. 259 Cover the mechanical with a tissue.

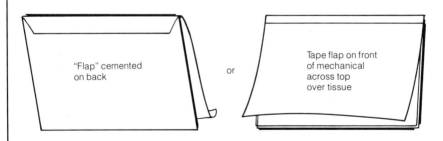

"Flap" cemented on back

or

Tape flap on front of mechanical across top over tissue

Fig. 260 "Flap" the mechanical with a heavier paper (black or color).

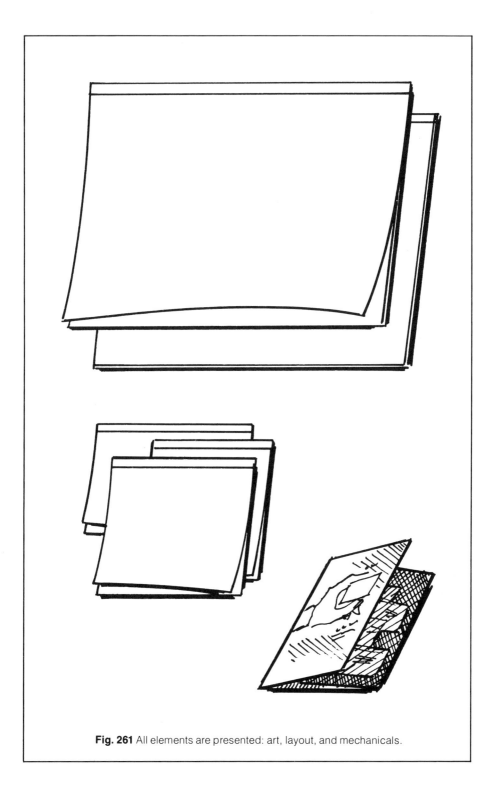

Fig. 261 All elements are presented: art, layout, and mechanicals.

CHAPTER 10

FROM LAYOUT TO MECHANICAL

To EXERCISE some of the information covered in previous chapters, let us now discuss two typical layouts and possible approaches to their mechanical assembly.

COMBINATION WITH DROP-OUT AND SURPRINT
The magazine ad layout shown in Fig. 262 is composed of eight elements—two headlines, a subhead, text, logo, address line, and two photos. Mechanical preparation would be as follows.

Rule the mechanical to the dimensions of the trim size of the magazine page, then rule the dimensions of the inside "live area" (the area to contain the elements of the ad).

Have a matte positive photostat made of each photo to the size shown in the layout (Fig. 263). Cement them in position on the mechanical and trim them accurately.

Have a glossy negative photostat made of the headline to be dropped out (Fig. 264). Cut it out (not too close to the type) and cement it in position directly on the photostat of the photograph.

If the headline for the black surprint is the correct size, cut it out and cement it onto the photostat of the photograph. If it is not the correct size, have it photostatted to reproduction size and cement the stat on the mechanical.

Paste up the subhead and text (Fig. 265). Rule in the line to appear over the address. Paste up the address. Use glossy photostats or direct positives of the type if sizes must be changed.

Have a glossy stat or direct positive made of the logo and paste it in position (Fig. 266).

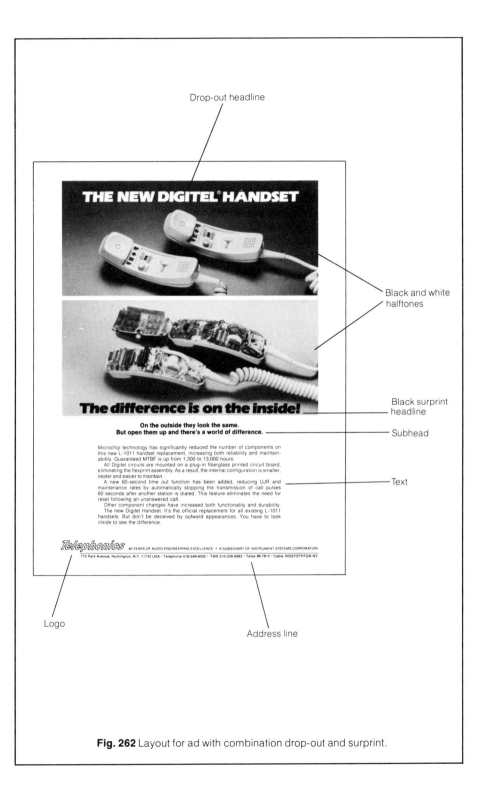

Drop-out headline

Black and white halftones

Black surprint headline

Subhead

Text

Logo

Address line

Fig. 262 Layout for ad with combination drop-out and surprint.

149

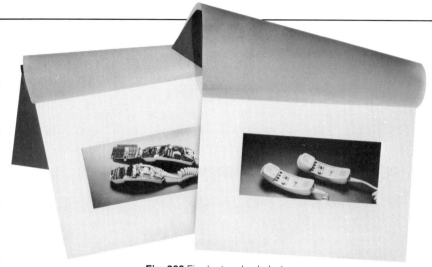

Fig. 263 Final retouched photos.

Fig. 264 Glossy negative stat of headline, repro size.

Fig. 265 Type proof.

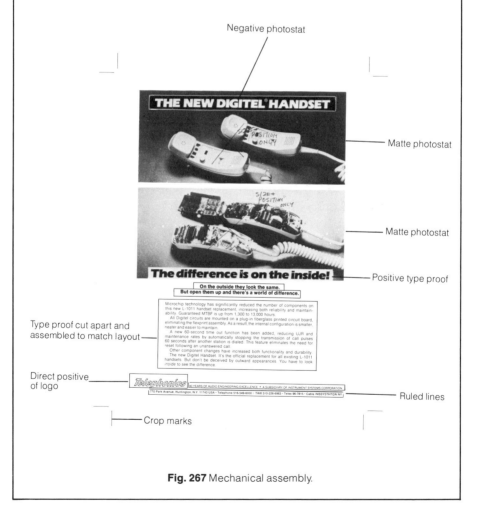

Fig. 266 Master logo and direct positive, repro size.

Negative photostat

Matte photostat

Matte photostat

Positive type proof

Type proof cut apart and assembled to match layout

Direct positive of logo

Ruled lines

Crop marks

Fig. 267 Mechanical assembly.

After all elements have been pasted up neatly, tape a piece of vellum or tracing paper over the mechanical and write on it your instructions to the platemaker. Bracket the top headline and write, "This type to drop out of black and white halftone." Bracket the bottom headline and write, "This type to surprint black and white halftone." Lift the tissue and write on each photostat, "For size and position. Strip in black halftone from original photo." The mechanical is now complete (Fig. 267).

TWO COLORS
As simple as this layout for a brochure cover appears, it lends itself quite nicely to some variety. For example, it is to be printed in two colors as indicated in Fig. 268.

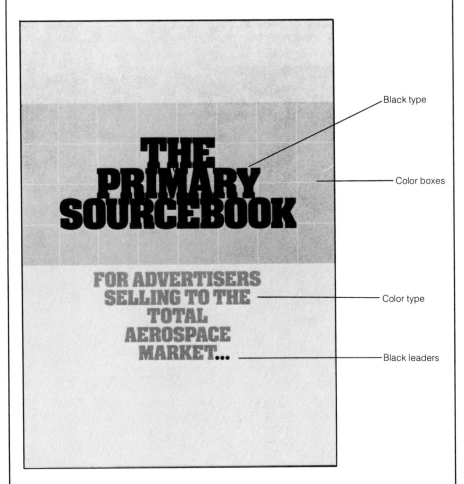

Fig. 268 Layout for a two-color brochure cover.

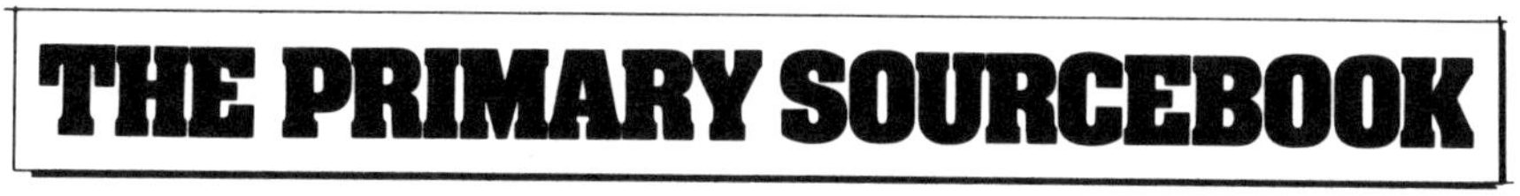

THE PRIMARY SOURCEBOOK

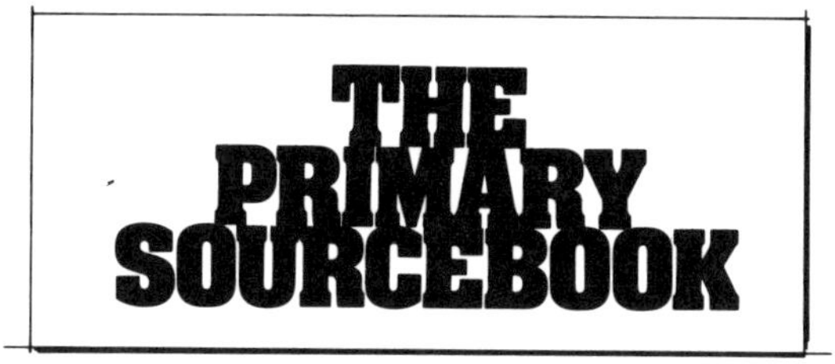

Fig. 269 Photo headline: as set (above), and cut apart and rearranged according to the layout.

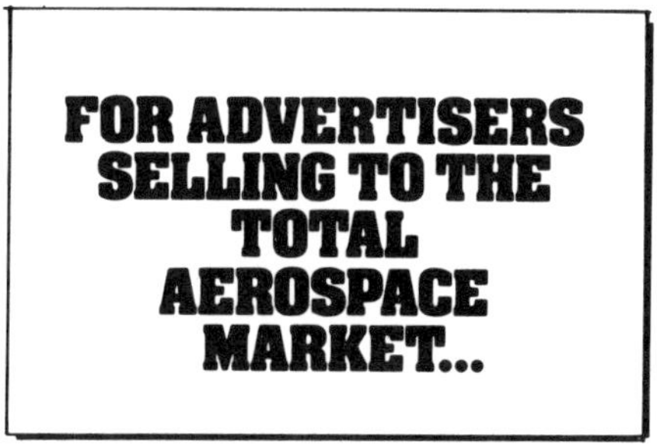

Fig. 270 Type proof.

Rule the dimensions for the cover (8½″ × 11″) and indicate the corner crop marks and fold marks (left vertical). The headline is set in photo headline strips; that is to say, it is set in a continuous line, not as shown in the layout. You will have to cut it apart and arrange it according to the layout (Fig. 269). This can be done on a separate piece of ledger bond paper; the type is then cut out as one assembled unit, called a "patch," which can be manipulated and positioned with ease during mechanical preparation. If this headline type is not the correct reproduction size, you can have a glossy positive or direct positive made to the required size.

Next, you might check the subhead for size and arrangement. This phototype could have been set in the actual size and arrangement of the layout (Fig. 270). If so, simply cut it out neatly and cement it into position on the mechanical. If not, cut it apart and paste it up in its proper arrangement. This can be done either directly in position on the mechanical or on a separate patch, cut out and cemented into position on the mechanical.

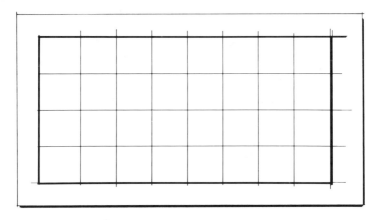

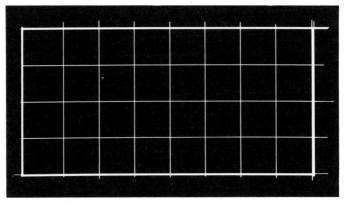

Fig. 271 Original art (above) and glossy negative of grid.

In order to create the grid background art, pencil the shape on fine-quality, smooth-surfaced white illustration board or drawing paper and simply ink the white lines in *black*. Be certain your ink work is clean and black. Then send the grid line art out for a glossy first print photostat. The result will be the opposite of the original—white lines on a black background (Fig. 271). Cut this stat to proper size and cement it on the mechanical.

Now place register marks on the board, one on each side and at the bottom outside the trim lines. Position a sheet of clear acetate over the mechanical. Tape it securely across the top edge of the board and place the corresponding register marks on it to align perfectly with those on the board. Now cement the headline assembly patch on the acetate overlay. The mechanical is now complete (Fig. 272).

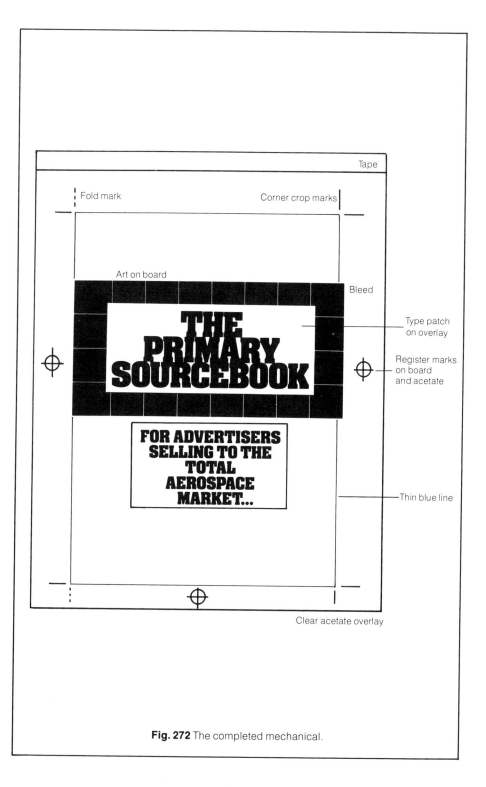

Fig. 272 The completed mechanical.

Production instructions would be as follows: on the board you would write (neatly and legibly), "Blue plate". On the overlay: "This overlay to print 100% black over 100% blue." Inasmuch as it is difficult to write on acetate, you can place a small piece of white or tan tape in the corner and write your instructions on it.

Now consider this mechanical assembly for a moment. Without changing it, but by changing the instructions, you can get a lot of mileage out of it.

For example, the grid background can be changed to a screened tint of blue instead of solid. All you have to do is point to it and write, "Art to print 40% blue."

You might decide that a checkerboard pattern would do nicely and change your instructions. This would be done on a tissue color break over the mechanical. Fill in the light and dark boxes with markers as you want them to appear, and write instructions to print them in 40% blue and solid blue.

Another variation would be to transpose the colors and print the headline in blue and the grid in black. This, of course, would not work because you could not read the blue over the black (inks are transparent). So you might lighten the background by having it screened to about 30% or 40% black. This can be accomplished by indicating on your tissue color break that the headline is to print solid blue (also change the instructions on the overlay itself) and the background to print 30% black. Bear in mind that the transparent blue ink will change color when printed over the screen of black.

Actually, if you wanted to have blue type on a black background it could be done by indicating it as such with markers on the color break tissue along with the following instructions: "Type to drop out of black plate and imprint solid blue." The type will first be dropped out of the black grid and printed as white type on black. The blue type, which is the same size as the white type, is then printed over the white. This gives the effect of blue type printed on a black background.

One more possibility would be to change it to a one-color job—black. The headline prints solid black over a screened background (surprint), and the subhead prints a screen of black (gray) as well. Indicate it as such on a tissue and write the instructions: "Black type to surprint 40% black." Point to the subhead: "Type to print 70% black." Point to the leaders (three dots): "Leaders print 100% black."

All this is done without changing the mechanical, just the instructions. This should serve as an example of coordination of production knowledge and mechanical preparation. The more you know of production, the easier it is to decide on the preparation. And the more you know of preparation, the easier it is to create an effect.

Do not rely on these simple examples alone. Study magazines and newspaper advertisements; examine with a professional eye the mailing pieces you receive at home. Ask yourself how you would have prepared the mechanical for this ad, or how that particular effect was achieved. Why did the designer approach it this way; why not another arrangement? Perhaps the budget prevented the use of screens or a second color. On the other hand, the simplicity of an approach and intelligent use of available facilities may be the very things that make a particular ad outstanding. Remember: the effect is the result of advertising know-how. Good luck.

INDEX